MESSAGE OF THE FATHERS OF THE CHURCH
General Editor: Thomas Halton

Volume 8

MINISTRY

by

Joseph T. Lienhard, S.J.

 Michael Glazier, Inc.
Wilmington, Delaware

ABOUT THE AUTHOR

JOSEPH T. LIENHARD, S.J. studied church history and patristics at the Universities of Mainz and Freiburg, where he received his doctorate. He is presently on the faculty of Marquette University. Among his publications is *Paulinus of Nola and Early Western Monasticism.*

First published in 1984 by Michael Glazier, Inc.
1723 Delaware Avenue, Wilmington, Delaware 19806

Library of Congress Catalog Card Number: 83-083154
International Standard Book Number:
  Message of the Fathers of the Church series:
  (0-89453-312-6, Paper; 0-89453-340-1, Cloth)
  MINISTRY
  (0-89453-320-7, Paper)
  (0-89453-348-7, Cloth)

Cover design: Lillian Brulc

We wish to acknowledge and thank the following for limited use of quotations from copyrighted works: Thomas Nelson Inc., for 11 quotations from *The Apostolic Fathers*, Jack N. Sparks, ed.; The Westminster Press, for 2 quotations from *Early Christian Fathers*, Cyril C. Richardson, ed., and for one quotation from *Early Latin Theology*, S.L. Greenslade, ed.; Clarendon Press for 4 quotations from *Didascalia Apostolorum*, R. Hugh Connolly, ed.; S.P.C.K. for 4 quotations from *Six Books on the Priesthood*, Graham Neville, ed., and for 2 quotations from *Homily on Baptism*, Ernest Evans, ed.; W. Heffer & Sons Limited for one quotation from *Commentary of Theodore of Mopsuestia on the Lord's Prayer and on the Sacraments of Baptism and the Eucharist*, A. Mingana, ed.; and Newman Press for one quotation from *Treatises on Penance*, William P LeSaint, ed.

Printed in the United States of America

CONTENTS

68174

EDITOR'S INTRODUCTION

The *Message of the Fathers of the Church* is a companion series to The *Old Testament Message* and The *New Testament Message*. It was conceived and planned in the belief that Scripture and Tradition worked hand in hand in the formation of the thought, life and worship of the primitive Church. Such a series, it was felt, would be a most effective way of opening up what has become virtually a closed book to present-day readers, and might serve to stimulate a revival in interest in Patristic studies in step with the recent, gratifying resurgence in Scriptural studies.

The term "Fathers" is usually reserved for Christian writers marked by orthodoxy of doctrine, holiness of life, ecclesiastical approval and antiquity. "Antiquity" is generally understood to include writers down to Gregory the Great (+604) or Isidore of Seville (+636) in the West, and John Damascene (+749) in the East. In the present series, however, greater elasticity has been encouraged, and quotations from writers not noted for orthodoxy will sometimes be included in order to illustrate the evolution of the Message on particular doctrinal matters. Likewise, writers later than the mid-eighth century will sometimes be used to illustrate the continuity of tradition on matters like sacramental theology or liturgical practice.

An earnest attempt was made to select collaborators on a broad inter-disciplinary and inter-confessional basis, the chief consideration being to match scholars who could handle the Fathers in their original languages with subjects in which they had already demonstrated a special interest and competence. About the only editorial directive given to the selected contributors was that the Fathers, for the most part, should be allowed to speak for themselves and that

7

they should speak in readable, reliable modern English. Volumes on individual themes were considered more suitable than volumes devoted to individual Fathers, each theme, hopefully, contributing an important segment to the total mosaic of the Early Church, one, holy, catholic and apostolic. Each volume has an introductory essay outlining the historical and theological development of the theme, with the body of the work mainly occupied with liberal citations from the Fathers in modern English translation and a minimum of linking commentary. Short lists of Suggested Further Readings are included; but dense, scholarly footnotes were actively discouraged on the pragmatic grounds that such scholarly shorthand has other outlets and tends to lose all but the most relentlessly esoteric reader in a semipopular series.

At the outset of his *Against Heresies* Irenaeus of Lyons warns his readers "not to expect from me any display of rhetoric, which I have never learned, or any excellence of composition, which I have never practised, or any beauty or persuasiveness of style, to which I make no pretensions." Similarly, modest disclaimers can be found in many of the Greek and Latin Fathers and all too often, unfortunately, they have been taken at their word by an uninterested world. In fact, however, they were often highly educated products of the best rhetorical schools of their day in the Roman Empire, and what they have to say is often as much a lesson in literary and cultural, as well as in spiritual, edification.

St. Augustine, in *The City of God* (19.7), has interesting reflections on the need for a common language in an expanding world community; without a common language a man is more at home with his dog than with a foreigner as far as intercommunication goes, even in the Roman Empire, which imposes on the nations it conquers the yoke of both law and language with a resultant abundance of interpreters. It is hoped that in the present world of continuing language barriers the contributors to this series will prove opportune interpreters of the perennial Christian message.

Thomas Halton

PREFACE

When Professor Thomas Halton invited me to edit this volume, I saw two goals as particularly important. One was choosing texts that were long enough to convey a sense of the author's style and theological outlook. This was not always easy, since the Fathers did not often write extensively about ministry; but to present only a sentence or two at a time is to make them speak our message, not theirs. The other goal was including some texts from the later Fathers, so that the volume would show more than just the earliest development of ministry. The meager texts on ministry in the New Testament and the Apostolic Fathers have been studied elsewhere and often with admirable thoroughness, whereas texts illustrating the later developments of ministry are not so readily available.

Among other themes, I have tried to choose some passages which portray the activities of the ministry—preaching, teaching, admonishing, celebrating the liturgy. In selecting these texts, I have been surprised at how much the Fathers were concerned with the moral guidance and correction of their congregations, and how little they say about the celebration of the liturgy (although Chrysostom and Theodore of Mopsuestia are exceptions to this). Other texts were chosen because they show some of the difficulties and problems of the ministry, or because they discuss the priesthood of all believers or the role of the laity in clerical elections, or because they illustrate the qualification of the clerical state by celibacy or common life.

Eight of the passages are from translations already published, and are marked as such. The other ten are my own translations. The key terms *episkopos, presbyteros, hiereus* and *diakonos* in Greek, and their Latin equivalents *episcopus, presbyter* or *senior, sacerdos* and *diaconus* have consistently been translated "bishop," "presbyter," "priest" and "deacon." This is true even in biblical passages in which, if they were quoted in a different context, this might not be the most obvious translation. The Fathers generally use "priest" both of bishops and of presbyters. Quotations from the Bible are uniformly identified by chapter and verse according to the Revised Standard Version with the Apocrypha, but may differ markedly from that translation, since the ancient author's own text is translated.

Finally, I am very grateful to Miss Camille Slowinski for typing the final draft of this volume so well, and to Gregory Sobolewski for valuable help with proofreading.

Marquette University, Milwaukee

August 28, 1983
Memorial of Saint Augustine

INTRODUCTION

"Ministry" means "service." Luke's gospel records Jesus' saying, "I am among you as one who serves" [Luke 22:27]. And in Mark's gospel Jesus recommends his example to his followers: "Whoever would be great among you must be your servant, and whoever would be first among you must be the slave of all. For the Son of man also came not to be served but to serve" [Mark 10:43-45]. The noun "ministry" began to be used as a technical term as early as St. Paul's letter to the Romans, where he speaks of his ministry as an apostle to the Gentiles [Rom 11:13]. In Acts 1:25 Matthias is elected to a "ministry and apostleship" to replace Judas. In the pastoral Epistles, Timothy is told: "Do the work of an evangelist, fulfill your ministry" [2 Tim 4:5].

As a technical term, the word "ministry" does two things: It designates a function or office in the Christian community or church, and it describes the attitude with which that function or office should be fulfilled. Ministry is a function or office, and in this sense carries with it some sort of authority; a paid servant need not be told to be like one who serves. But by choosing the word "ministry" to describe office in the church, the second-generation Christians were faithful to the memory of Jesus' own words; instead of using available words like "power" or "authority," they gave the word "ministry" a new and specifically Christian meaning.

The New Testament

The topic of this anthology is ministry in the early Church, not in the New Testament. Still, the New Testament cannot be ignored. The New Testament writings are the oldest written records of Christianity, some composed as early as twenty years after Jesus' crucifixion. And then too, the Fathers of the Church—especially the later ones—go back time and time again to the New Testament to explain and justify their own understanding of ministry. Some of the most interesting passages in this anthology are those which explain and reinterpret biblical texts.

Ministry in the New Testament is characterized by diversity: the New Testament names many different ministries, and there is no way of reconciling them into one organizational system. Furthermore, while many titles are given, we are not always sure of their functions.

The most familiar and most important ministry in the New Testament is the apostleship. Perhaps sixteen or seventeen men in the New Testament are accorded the title "apostle," so that "apostles" are not simply identical with "the Twelve." An apostle is one who is sent, and sent primarily to preach or proclaim the Gospel. Paul, for example, considers both Peter and himself apostles [Gal 2:7-9]. Not all apostles travelled; James the son of Zebedee appears to have remained in Jerusalem, where he was martyred in A.D. 44. Others besides the Twelve who are called apostles are Barnabas, Silvanus, Andronicus and Junias.

Paul lists other ministries, too: writing to the church in Corinth, he enumerates apostles, prophets, teachers, workers of miracles, healers, helpers, administrators, and speakers in various kinds of tongues [1 Cor 12:28]. The epistle to the Ephesians lists apostles, prophets, evangelists, pastors and teachers [Eph 4:11].

The Acts of the Apostles records—perhaps in light of later experience—how the Christians of Jerusalem solved a conflict within the community by establishing a new ministry or office: because of disputes about the distribution of alms, seven men were ordained to oversee this work [Acts

6:1-6]. Luke refers to them by the collective title "the Seven" [Acts 21:8]; later Christians saw in this passage the institution of the diaconate.

Paul, in his letter to the Philippians, is the first to use two titles together which later became standard. The letter is addressed to the church at Philippi, "with the bishops and deacons" (the phrase could just as well be translated "with the overseers and servers"). In any case, these titles were gradually adopted as standard, and the pastoral Epistles give extended instructions on the qualities requisite for these ministries [see 1 Tim 3:1-13; Titus 1:5-9].

"Bishops" could be called "presbyters," or "elders," but "presbyter" was sometimes used for a distinct office. The Greek word *presbyteros* has come in to English twice: directly, as "presbyter,"and indirectly, as "priest." But these two English words are now used—here and generally—to translate two different words in Greek and Latin. "Presbyter" (or "elder") is used for *presbyteros* or *senior*, "priest" for *hiereus* or *sacerdos.* It is worth noting that the word *hiereus* or "priest" in the New Testament is used of Christ, of Jewish religious officials, and of the whole Christian people, but not of specific members of the Christian community; this usage began only later.

Omitting much else, we can say in summary that the New Testament shows a wide variety of ministries or offices in the earliest communities. What is quite certain is that Christian communities had established patterns of leadership. The probability is that the leadership was, in theory at least, permanent, so that the use of the term "office" is justified.

After the New Testament

One of the most intriguing developments in the early church is the transition from the New Testament plurality of ministries to a more or less uniform and fixed structure. The transition was essentially completed by the middle of the second century, in almost all the churches of the Empire. There is hardly unanimity on even a single point on this topic; what follows is—I hope—at least a probable picture. The Christian Gospel was proclaimed by apostles, and more generally by persons who served as part-time missionaries. Their task, as they saw it, was to proclaim the Gospel and baptize those who accepted it; they would then organize a community and move on. Some kind of leadership in these communities was necessary. One of the most important influences in the development of the Christian churches was the practice of assembling each Sunday for reading, teaching, the celebration of the Eucharist, and an *agape* or church supper, or some smaller combination of these four elements. At the very least, such a weekly assembly required organization, and, if teaching was to take place, some education.

In the first decades of development, however, the real leadership was apparently in the hands of men who visited the communities only occasionally and irregularly; they might be called apostles, or prophets, or teachers. This system gave rise to difficulties: the apostle or prophet or teacher was often absent; and unworthy men or even charlatans began to assume these roles. A glance at the concordance to the New Testament and the Apostolic Fathers under the prefix *pseudo-* or "false" is revealing and sobering: Christianity, in its first century, knew false apostles, false prophets, and false teachers with some frequency.

The *Didache* [#3] shows with striking clarity the need for a change: the author knows "apostles" and "prophets" who are free-loaders, and provides his communities with fairly elaborate rules for treating these persons well but at the same time avoiding being duped. Toward the end of his little manual, he urges his communities to choose for themselves bishops and deacons, and to honor them like apostles and prophets. This suggests that local leadership was considerably less romantic, and the people somewhat reluctant to accept it. To elect as bishop the local butcher or school-teacher had its drawbacks, but it did provide stable and responsible leadership by people known to the community.

Again, this is another point of widely divergent interpretation: but in general, it seems that Jewish-Christian communities were led by a group of presbyters or elders, while

Gentile-Christian communities were led by "bishops" and "deacons," with the bishops sometimes also called presbyters or elders. This latter constitution is found in Paul's letter to the Philippians, 1 Timothy, *1 Clement* [#1], and the *Didache* [#3]. The evidence for government by elders is clearest in Acts 11:30; 14:23; 20:17-38; 21:18; Jas 5:14; 1 Pet 5:1-4.

Eventually, the two systems gave way to a new structure, first evident in Ignatius of Antioch [#2], ca. 110. The head of the community was a single bishop (the institution of the monepiscopate), and all authority ultimately rested with him (therefore the "monarchical episcopate"). The presbyters acted as his advisers, and acted together; there is a collective noun, *presbytērion* or presbytery, to designate them as a group. The deacons' function was primarily to carry out the social works of charity designated by the bishop. In modern terms, the bishop was more like a pastor, because a "church" was (in the early second century) all the Christians of a city or town. The presbyters together acted like a parish council, although Ignatius suggests that in the bishop's absence one of the presbyters could act in his place and preside at the Eucharist. The deacons' work was principally practical, but very important. The early church maintained an elaborate and admirable system of charity for the maintenance of widows, orphans, and other needy persons.

We cannot assume that all churches had the structure found in Ignatius. From evidence in the *Shepherd* of Hermas, for example, it would seem that the monarchical episcopate was not established at Rome until after A.D. 140 or so. But the monepiscopate seems to have spread to most churches by the middle of the second century.

More importantly, the number of functions carried out by the bishop grew. He was the liturgical leader of the community, admitting candidates to baptism and presiding at the Eucharist; he was the teacher and moral guide of the community; he received guests from other churches, and maintained his church "in communion" with other churches; he ordained presbyters and deacons, and could therefore control who was ordained; and finally, he participated in the ordination of other bishops. As Ignatius portrays it, and as later became the case everywhere, he was responsible for the orthodoxy of his community, and could refuse to be in communion with—that is, excommunicate—a person whom he believed to be in error.

With the growth of the communities, new offices or ministries were established. One important one, in the East, was that of deaconess, as a passage from the *Didascalia apostolorum*, and other texts, show [#6; 10]. Both in East and West, various "minor orders" also evolved. The church historian, Eusebius, quotes Cornelius of Rome, who described the church there around the year 250: "one bishop,. . . forty-six presbyters, seven deacons, seven subdeacons, forty-two acolytes, fifty-two exorcists, readers, and doorkeepers, and more than fifteen hundred widows and distressed persons" [*Ecclesiastical History* 6, 43, 11].

Theological Developments: The Use of the Old Testament

It is not wholly right to speak of a "theology" of ministry in the second, third, and fourth centuries; nevertheless, the ministry was explained in new ways, and ways that went beyond the merely practical.

One important influence on development of thought about ministry was the Old Testament. Once having accepted the Jewish scriptures as their own, through a Christological understanding of the Old Testament, Christians read the Old Testament—at the Sunday liturgy, particularly—and sought in it not only the history of God's acts in the past but also a better understanding of their own place in the history of salvation. The Christological interpretation of the Old Testament began very early; once this was established, understanding of the Church and even its worship and ministry was also sought in the Old Testament.

The argument took different forms. Clement of Rome [#1] argues that the New Covenant is more perfect than the Old; if therefore the clergy of the Old Covenant were

ordered and disciplined, so much the more should those of
the New Covenant be. The author of the *Didache* [#3] was
the first to apply Mal 1:11 ("From the rising of the sun to its
setting my name has been glorified among the Gentiles, and
in every place incense and a pure sacrifice is offered to my
name") to the Christian Eucharist. The Eucharist is thus
called a sacrifice; and this easily leads to calling the president of the Eucharistic assembly a priest. Something new is
present here. Clement merely argues that the new order
must be like the old but surpass it; the author of the *Didache*
takes the text from Malachi as a prophecy of the Eucharist.
Still another relationship is found in the ordination prayers
in Hippolytus [#5], which presuppose a continuity between
the Old Testament events and the Christian ministry. In the
passages translated below, other ways of applying the Old
Testament to Christian ministry are represented; one particularly interesting example is Origen's *Homilies on Leviticus*
[#7].

Theological Developments: Apostolic Succession

With the multiplication of dissident interpretations of
Christianity in the second century, the need for a criterion of
truth or orthodoxy was pressing. The newly-formed New
Testament was not adequate, since Gnostics and others were
interpreting it in their own favor. Thus there arose the
concept of "apostolic succession." Irenaeus of Lyons, for
example, argues that the apostles appointed bishops for the
important cities, and taught these bishops the fullness of
truth. These bishops in turn taught their successors, so that
anyone who sought the truth could consult the bishop of
one of the sees founded by the apostles [*Against the Heresies*
3, 3, 1]. A further development is seen in Cyprian, who
practically identifies bishops—all bishops—with the apostles. He writes, for example, to Florentius, "You appoint
yourself a judge of God and of Christ, who says to the
apostles and thus to all those rulers who now succeed to the
apostles by delegated ordination: 'He who hears you hears

me'" [*Letter* 66, 4]. The bishops, therefore, enjoy in their churches the same authority as the original apostles and are able—among other things—to interpret the Bible authoritatively.

Constitutional Developments

The relation of bishops to one another, and their relation to the larger catholic or universal church, also developed rapidly. From the end of the second century, the bishops of a region began to meet in synods at times of crisis, in order to discuss matters of doctrine or discipline. The first ecumenical council of bishops met at Nicaea in 325. Furthermore, in the eastern Empire especially, the system of church provinces grew up: the bishop of the capital city of a political province began to enjoy certain rights and precedence over the other bishops of that province, especially the right to approve candidates for vacant bishoprics in the province. The bishops of these capital cities became known as metropolitans or (later in the West) as archbishops. In Egypt, the bishop of the port city of Alexandria had the role of metropolitan for all the bishops of the cities along the Nile. In the West, the development did not follow the lines of political provinces; instead, the bishops of the two largest cities, Rome and Carthage, became the leaders of the churches in Italy and North Africa, respectively. The Council of Nicaea (A.D. 325) marked a further step: the bishops of three cities (Alexandria, Antioch, and Rome) were recognized as patriarchs, with jurisdiction over larger areas or groups of provinces. Later councils added Constantinople and Jerusalem to the list of patriarchates. Two principles were established: the collegiality of all bishops, and the ordering of local churches into larger units of ecclesiastical jurisdiction.

The Relations of Bishops, Presbyters and Deacons

The earliest role of the presbyters was apparently that of adviser to the bishop, and perhaps of liturgical president in the bishop's absence. The phenomenon of the presbyter as the regular, independent celebrant of the Eucharist is found first in the third century. A letter of Dionysius of Alexandria (quoted in Eusebius's *Ecclesiastical History* 7, 24, 6) suggests that presbyters presided over village congregations in Egypt by the middle of the third century. Cyprian, in *Letter* 18, allows presbyters and even deacons to reconcile sinners in times of persecution, a function which had previously been reserved to the bishop. In a large city like Rome, once no one building could hold all the Christians at one time, houses (called *tituli*) were purchased around the city and used for the Eucharist on Sunday, as well as for residences for presbyters and deacons, thus multiplying the number of parishes.

Canon 13 of the synod of Ancyra (ca. 315, in Asia Minor) is typical of a further development: it forbids the ordination of bishops for small villages, and prescribes that presbyters should be assigned to them. Gradually, therefore, in the third and fourth centuries, presbyters came to function as pastors of local churches, and the older practice of all the Christians of a city forming one "parish" disappeared [see #12].

Conflict among the orders was not absent, as several texts below show. Deacons, perhaps because they were responsible for distributing money and goods, sometimes gained too much power and became rebellious [#14]. And a few fourth- and fifth-century authors discuss the relation between bishops and presbyters—and two at least, John Chrysostom and Jerome [#10; 16], see little difference between them.

The Clerical State

In the course of time, various requirements or conditions for admission to the Christian clergy evolved, and the clergy came to enjoy certain privileges or distinctions, as well as—in some cases—to be subjected to certain restrictions.

The requirements or conditions for admission to the clergy were never uniform; nevertheless, some patterns are clear. In many churches, a certain age was specified for admission to an order. Pope Zozimus (417-418), for example, specified the minimum age of 21 for subdeacons, 25 for deacons, and 30 for presbyters. Corporeal integrity, except in the case of those who were tortured in persecutions, was also often required. The performance of public penance (allowed only once in a lifetime) generally excluded a man from any clerical order, as did the condition of slavery. (The latter restriction was imposed by imperial law.) Gregory of Nazianzus [#18], writes eloquently of the intellectual and spiritual preparation which a cleric needs.

Celibacy was never an absolute requirement for ordination in the early church. But Tertullian and Origen both admired voluntary clerical continence, on the grounds that the prayers of the continent are more effective, and that this purity befits the celebration of the mysteries. But the only demand usually made on clerics was that they marry only once; the phrase from the pastoral Epistles, "the husband of one wife" [1 Tim 3:2, 12; Titus 1:6], was often the point of departure for discussions of this topic. Eventually, East and West came to differ. The East finally demanded continence only of bishops, and according to a conciliar decree of 692 a married man who was elected a bishop had to separate himself from his wife and put her into a convent. In the West, from the late fourth century onwards, the Roman bishops began to insist that from the time of his ordination to the diaconate a man must abstain from relations with his wife. The documents presuppose that the couple already has children, and that the family will remain together [for example, #18].

A few attempts were made at having the clergy live common life, that is, to surrender the ownership of private property and to live in one house. Eusebius of Vercelli (d. 371) and Augustine attempted this. The failure of Augustine's effort is documented below [#17].

Both in the case of celibacy and of common life, the influence of the rapidly spreading monastic movement on the clergy is clear.

From the time of Constantine on, the Christian clergy

were granted certain privileges by the imperial government. One of the earliest and most important was freedom from certain burdensome taxes. Another—questionable— privilege was the right of a Christian bishop to adjudicate a civil case if both parties agreed to his hearing it. This soon became a burden for the bishops of larger cities, and Augustine complains of spending several hours some days settling lawsuits between Christians. Eventually, bishops and other clerics were assigned ranks within the imperial aristocracy. On the other hand, imperial legislation also had to restrain clerics occasionally, as Jerome's allusion to an imperial edict forbidding Christian clergy to hunt for legacies [#16] shows. Imperial legislation affecting the clergy became increasingly frequent in the late fourth century and after, and was one factor in the development of a clerical class in society.

ABBREVIATIONS

ACW   Ancient Christian Writers

CCL   Corpus Christianorum, series latina (Turnhout)

CSEL Corpus scriptorum ecclesiasticorum latinorum
      (Vienna)

GCS   Die griechischen christlichen Schriftsteller der
      ersten Jahrhunderte (Berlin)

PG   Migne, Patrologia Graeca

PL   Migne, Patrologia Latina

SC   Sources chrétiennes (Paris)

1. THE EARLY DEVELOPMENT

1. The First Epistle of Clement, 40-44

[Tr. by Holt H. Graham]

The *First Epistle of Clement* was addressed by the church in Rome to the church in Corinth, and written ca. A.D. 96. "Clement" was traditionally considered its author, although his name never appears in the letter. The occasion was unrest in the Corinthian church: some younger members had rebelled against the elders or presbyters there and forced them out of office. The purpose of the letter is to urge their reinstatement on the Corinthian Christians. In the passage which follows, the author uses the Old Testament to argue for order in the Christian communities. The passage also contains one of the earliest teachings on succession; the author sees the bishops' authority derived ultimately from their appointment by the apostles. The letter presupposes that the churches are governed by two groups, bishops (always in the plural) and deacons; the bishops are also called "presbyters."

40.[1] Now then, since this is quite plain to us, and we have gained insight into the depths of the divine knowledge, we

[1]Text: SC 167.166-174, ed. by A. Jaubert (1971). Trans.: *The Apostolic Fathers. Volume 2: First and Second Clement,* by Robert M. Grant and Holt H. Graham, (Camden, 1965), 68-74.

ought to do in order all those things the Master has ordered us to perform at the appointed times. 2. He has commanded sacrifices and services to be performed, not in a careless and haphazard way but at the designated seasons and hours. 3. He himself has determined where and through whom he wishes them performed, to the intent that everything should be done religiously to his good pleasure and acceptably to his will. 4. Those then who offer their sacrifices at the appointed seasons are acceptable and blessed; for since they comply with the Master's orders, they do not sin. 5. Thus to the high priest have been appointed his proper services, to the priests their own place assigned, upon the Levites their proper duties imposed; and the layman is bound by the rules for laymen.

41. Each of us, brethren, in his own rank must please God in good conscience, not overstepping the fixed rules of his ministry, and with reverence. 2. Not everywhere, brethren, but in Jerusalem only are the perpetual sacrifices offered, whether thank offering or those for sin and trespass; and even there they are not offered in every place, but only in front of the sanctuary, at the altar, after the offering has been inspected by the high priest and the aforementioned ministers. 3. Further, those who do anything contrary to the duty imposed by his will incur the death penalty. 4. Understand then, brethren: the greater the knowledge that has been bestowed upon us, the greater the risk we run.

42. The apostles received the gospel for us from Jesus Christ, and Jesus the Christ was sent from God. 2. So Christ is from God, and the apostles are from Christ: thus both came in proper order by the will of God. 3. And so the apostles, after they had received their orders and in full assurance by reason of the resurrection of our Lord Jesus Christ, being full of faith in the word of God, went out in the conviction of the Holy Spirit preaching the good news that God's kingdom was about to come. 4. So as they preached from country to country and from city to city, they appointed their first converts, after testing them by the Spirit, to be the bishops and deacons of the future believers.

5. Nor was this an innovation; since bishops and deacons had been written of long before. For thus says the Scripture somewhere, "I will appoint their bishops in righteousness and their deacons in faith" [cf. Isa 60:17].

43. And is it any wonder, if those who in Christ were entrusted by God with such a duty should appoint those just mentioned? For when the blessed Moses, too, "a faithful servant in all the house" [Num 12:7] wrote in the sacred books all that had been commanded him, the rest of the prophets became his successors to testify with him to his legislation. 2. For he himself, when strife arose over the priesthood and the tribes were in rebellion over the question which one of them should be adorned with the glorious title, commanded the twelve tribal chiefs to bring to him the staffs inscribed with the name of each tribe. The he took them and tied them together and sealed them with the rings of the chiefs, and deposited them in the tent of the testimony on the table of God. 3. Then when he had shut the tent he sealed the keys as he had the staffs, 4. and said to the chiefs, "Men and brethren, the tribe whose staff buds is the one God has chosen for his priesthood and ministry." 5. So early in the morning he summoned all Israel, six hundred thousand men, and showed the seals to the tribal chiefs and opened the tent of the testimony and produced the staffs; and the staff of Aaron was found not only to have budded but to be bearing fruit. 6. What do you think, beloved? did not Moses know in advance that this would happen? Of course he knew. But he acted as he did lest there be an insurrection in Israel and in order that the name of the true and only God might be glorified; to whom be the glory for ever and ever. Amen.

44. And our apostles knew through our Lord Jesus Christ that there would be strife over the title of bishop. 2. So for this reason, because they had been given full foreknowledge, they appointed those mentioned above and afterward added the stipulation that if these should die, other approved men should succeed to their ministry. 3. Those therefore who were appointed by them or afterward by other reputable men with the consent of the whole Church, who in humility have ministered to the flock of Christ blamelessly, quietly, and unselfishly, and who have long been approved by all— these men we consider are being unjustly removed from their ministry. 4. Surely we will be guilty of no small sin if we thrust out of the office of bishop those who have offered the gifts in a blameless and holy fashion. 5. Blessed indeed are the presbyters who have already passed on, who had a fruitful and perfect departure, for they need not be concerned lest someone remove them from the place established for them. 6. But you, we observe, have removed some who were conducting themselves well from the ministry they have irreproachably honored.

2. Ignatius of Antioch
Letters (excerpts)

[Tr. by Robert M. Grant]

Ignatius was bishop of Antioch at the beginning of the second century. Sometime around A.D. 110 he was condemned to death in Syria and transported to Rome to be thrown to the lions. While he was being brought through western Asia Minor, delegations from several Christian communities went to meet him, and he sent letters back to the communities. In his struggle against Gnostics and Judaizers, Ignatius laid great emphasis on unity in the church under the leadership of the bishop. He is one of the earliest witnesses to the monarchical episcopate, that is, to the practice of having one bishop at the head of a local church. The presbyters, for Ignatius, form a college to help the bishop, and they can be designated by a collective noun, *presbytery*. The deacons are the bishop's assistants. Ignatius does not mention succession from the apostles, but sees the earthly hierarchy as a reflection of the heavenly order.

LETTER TO THE EPHESIANS, 2, 2—6, 1

[2.][2] **2.** May I always have joy from you, if only I am worthy. It is fitting, then, in every way to glorify Jesus Christ, who glorified you, so that you may be made perfect in a single obedience to the bishop and the presbytery and be sanctified in every respect. **3.** I am not giving you commands as if I were someone. For even though I am in bonds for the Name, I am not yet perfect in Jesus Christ; for now I am beginning to be a disciple, and I speak to you as my fellow students. For I needed to be anointed by you with faith, instruction, endurance, patience. **2.** But since love does not let me be silent about you, I have undertaken to exhort you, so that together you may run your race in accordance with God's purpose. For Jesus Christ, our inseparable life, is the expressed purpose of the Father, just as the bishops who have been appointed throughout the world exist by the purpose of Jesus Christ.
4. Therefore it is fitting for you to run your race together with the bishop's purpose—as you do. For your presbytery—worthy of fame, worthy of God—is attuned to the bishop like strings to a lyre. Therefore by your unity and harmonious love Jesus Christ is sung. **2.** Each of you must be part of this chorus so that, being harmonious in unity, receiving God's pitch in unison, you may sing with one voice through Jesus Christ to the Father, so that he may both hear you and recognize you, through what you do well, as members of his Son. Therefore it is profitable for you to be in blameless unison, so that you may always participate in God.
5. For if in a short time I had such fellowship with your bishop as was not human but spiritual, how much more blessed do I consider you who are mingled with him as the Church is with Jesus Christ and as Jesus Christ is with the

---

[2]Text: SC 10.58-62, ed. by P. Th. Camelot (1969). Trans.: *The Apostolic Fathers. Volume 4: Ignatius of Antioch*, by Robert M. Grant, (Camden 1966) 33-37.

Father, so that all things are harmonious in unison! 2. Let no one deceive himself: unless a man is within the sanctuary, he lacks the bread of God. If the prayer of one or two has such power, how much more does that of the bishop and the whole church? 3. Therefore he who does not come to the assembly is already proud and has separated himself. For it is written, "God opposes the proud" [Prov 3:34]. Let us, therefore, be eager not to oppose the bishop, so that we may be subject to God.

6. And the more anyone sees the bishop being silent, the more one should fear him. For everyone whom the master of a house sends for his stewardship, we must receive as the one who sent him. It is obvious, then, that one must look upon the bishop as the Lord himself.

LETTER TO THE MAGNESIANS, 2-7; 13

2.[3] Since, then, I was judged worthy of seeing you through Damas your Godworthy bishop and the worthy presbyters Bassus and Apollonius and my fellow slave the deacon Zotion—whom may I enjoy because he is subject to the bishop as to God's grace and to the presbytery as to the law of Jesus Christ. . . .

3. And it is fitting for you not to take advantage of the bishop's youth but to render him full respect in accordance with the power of God the Father, just as I know that the holy presbyters have not presumed upon his youthful external appearance but, as men wise in God, yield to him—not to him but to the Father of Jesus Christ, to the bishop of all. 2. For the honor of him who loved us, it is fitting for us to obey without any hypocrisy; for a man does not deceive only this visible bishop but also cheats the invisible one. The reckoning of this account is not with flesh but with God, who knows men's secrets.

4. It is fitting, then, not just to be called Christians but to be such—just as some use the title "bishop" but do everything apart from him. Such men do not seem to me to act in

[3]Text: SC 10.84-86, 90. Trans.: Grant, 58-62,66.

good conscience, since they do not meet validly in accordance with the commandment.

5. Since, then, actions have a consequence and two goals lie before us, death and life, and each is going to go to his own place; 2. for just as there are two coinages, the one of God, the other of the world, and each has its own stamp impressed on it, unbelievers that of this world, believers (with love) the stamp of God the Father through Jesus Christ; and unless we voluntarily choose to die in relation to his passion, his life is not in us.

6. Since, then, in the persons already mentioned I have beheld the whole congregation in faith and have loved it, I exhort you: be eager to do everything in God's harmony, with the bishop presiding in the place of God and the presbytery in the place of the council of the apostles and the deacons, most sweet to me, entrusted with the service of Jesus Christ—who before the ages was with the Father and was made manifest at the end. 2. All of you, then, having received a divine agreement in your convictions, admonish one another, and let no one view his neighbor in a merely human way; but constantly love one another in Jesus Christ. Let there be nothing in you that can divide you, but be united with the bishop and with those who preside, for an example and lesson of imperishability.

7. As, then, the Lord did nothing apart from the Father, either by himself or through the apostles, since he was united with him, so you must do nothing apart from the bishop and the presbyters. Do not try to make anything appear praiseworthy by yourselves, but let there be in common one prayer, one petition, one mind, one hope in love, in blameless joy—which is Jesus Christ, than whom nothing is better. 2. All of you must run together as to one temple of God, as to one sanctuary, to one Jesus Christ, who proceeded from the one Father and is with the one and departed to the one.

13. Be eager, therefore, to be firmly set in the decrees of the Lord and the apostles so that "in whatever you do you may prosper" [Ps 1:3]—in flesh and spirit, in faith and love, in the Son and the Father and in the Spirit, at the beginning and at the end, together with your right reverend bishop and that worthily woven spiritual crown, your presbytery, and the godly deacons. 2. Be subject to the bishop and to one another, as Jesus Christ [in the flesh] was subject to the Father and the apostles were subject to Christ [and the Father], so that there may be unity both fleshly and spiritual.

LETTER TO THE TRALLIANS, 2-3; 7

2.[4] For when you subject yourselves to the bishop as to Jesus Christ, you appear to me to be living not in human fashion but like Jesus Christ, who died for us so that by believing in his death you might escape dying. 2. Therefore it is necessary that, as is actually the case, you do nothing apart from the bishop, but be subject also to the presbytery as to the apostles of Jesus Christ, our hope; for if we live in him we shall be found in him. 3. Those who are deacons of the mysteries of Jesus Christ must please all men in every way. For they are not ministers of food and drink but servants of the church of God; therefore they must guard themselves from accusations as from fire.

3. Similarly all are to respect the deacons as Jesus Christ and the bishop as a copy of the Father and the presbyters as the council of God and the band of the apostles. For apart from these no group can be called a church. 2. I am convinced that you accept this. For I have received an embodiment of your love, and have it with me, in your bishop, whose demeanor is a great lesson and whose gentleness is his power. I think that even the godless revere him.

7. Be on guard against such men. This will be the case for you if you are not puffed up but are inseparable from the God Jesus Christ and the bishop and the ordinances of the apostles. 2. He who is within the sanctuary is pure; he who is

---

[4]Text: SC 10.96, 100. Trans.: Grant, 72-73,76.

outside the sanctuary is not pure—that is, whoever does anything apart from the bishop and the presbytery and the deacons is not pure in conscience.

LETTER TO THE PHILADELPHIANS, 4-5; 7—8, 1

4.[5] Be eager, therefore, to use one Eucharist—for there is one flesh of our Lord Jesus Christ and one cup for union with his blood, one sanctuary, as there is one bishop, together with the presbytery and the deacons my fellow slaves—so that, whatever you do, you do it in relation to God. **5.** My brothers, I overflow with love for you, and I am exceedingly joyful to be watching out for your safety—not I, but Jesus Christ, for whom I am in bonds, though I fear all the more because I am still imperfect. But your prayer to God will make me perfect so that I may attain to the lot in which I was given mercy, fleeing to the gospel as to the flesh of Jesus and to the apostles as to the presbytery of the church. 2. The prophets we also love because they made a proclamation related to the gospel and set their hope on him and were waiting for him; by believing in him they were saved, being united with Jesus Christ. Worthy of love and admiration, they are saints, attested by Jesus Christ and numbered together with us in the gospel of the common hope.

7. For even if some desired to deceive me in a merely human way, the Spirit is not deceived, for it is from God. For it "knows whence it comes and whither it goes" [John 3:8] and exposes secrets. When I was with you I cried out, I spoke with a loud voice, God's own voice: "Pay attention to the bishop and the presbytery and deacons." 2. Some suspected me of saying this because I had advance information about the division of some persons; but he for whom I am in bonds is my witness that I did not know it from any human

[5]Text: SC 10.122-126. Trans.: Grant, 101-102, 104-105.

being. The Spirit made proclamation, saying this: "Do nothing apart from the bishop; keep your flesh as the temple of God; love unity; flee from divisions; be imitators of Jesus Christ as he is of his Father."

8. I did what I could as a man devoted to unity. But God does not dwell where there is division and wrath. The Lord forgives all who repent, if they repent and turn toward the unity of God and the council of the bishop. I am confident that by the grace of Jesus Christ he will loose every bond from you.

LETTER TO THE SMYRNAEANS, 8—9, 1

8.[6] All of you are to follow the bishop as Jesus Christ follows the Father, and the presbytery as the apostles. Respect the deacons as the command of God. Apart from the bishop no one is to do anything pertaining to the church. A valid Eucharist is to be defined as one celebrated by the bishop or by a representative of his. 2. Wherever the bishop appears, the whole congregation is to be present, just as wherever Jesus Christ is, there is the whole Church. It is not right either to baptize or to celebrate the agape[7] apart from the bishop; but whatever he approves is also pleasing to God—so that everything you do may be secure and valid.

9. Furthermore, it is reasonable for us to become sober while we still have time to repent toward God. It is good to know God and the bishop. He who honors the bishop has been honored by God; he who does anything without the bishop's knowledge worships the devil.

LETTER TO POLYCARP, 4-5

4.[8] Do not let the widows be neglected; after the Lord, you must be their guardian. Nothing is to be done without your

[6]Text: SC 10.138-140. Trans.: Grant, 120-121.

[7]The common religious meal which often accompanied the Eucharist in the early church; see 1 Cor 11:17-34.

[8]Text: SC 10.148-150. Trans.: Grant, 132-134.

approval, and you must do nothing without God—as indeed is your practice; stand firm. 2. Meetings should be more frequent; seek out all individually. 3. Do not be haughty toward slaves, whether men or women, but do not let them be puffed up. Let them be slaves, rather, for the glory of God, so that they may obtain a better freedom from God. They must not desire to be set free at the expense of the common fund, lest they be found to be slaves of lust.

5. Flee from evil arts, or indeed preach sermons about them. Tell my sisters to love the Lord and to be content with their husbands, both in flesh and in spirit. Similarly, in the name of Jesus Christ command my brothers to love their wives as the Lord loves the Church. 2. If anyone is able to remain in purity, in honor of the Lord's flesh, he must do so without boasting. If he boasts he is lost, and if it is made known to anyone but the bishop, he has been corrupted. It is fitting for men and women who marry to be united with the bishop's consent, so that the marriage may be related to the Lord, not to lust. Everything is to be done in God's honor.

3. Didache, 11-15

[Tr. by Cyril C. Richardson]

The *Didache*—its fuller title is *The Teaching of the Twelve Apostles*—is an anonymous church order which probably dates from the first half of the second century, and was edited perhaps in Syria or Palestine. The text is particularly interesting because it illustrates the reasons for a change in leadership from "apostles," "prophets," and "teachers" who visited Christian communities only irregularly to "bishops" and "deacons" who were members of the community and resided there permanently. The *Didache* also cites Mal 1:11 in reference to the Christian Eucharist, an important step in the development of the vocabulary of Christian priesthood.

11.[9] Now, you should welcome anyone who comes your way and teaches you all we have been saying. 2. But if the teacher proves himself a renegade and by teaching otherwise contradicts all this, pay no attention to him. But if his teaching furthers the Lord's righteousness and knowledge, welcome him as the Lord. 3. Now about the apostles and prophets: Act in line with the gospel precept. 4. Welcome every apostle on arriving, as if he were the Lord. 5. But he must not stay beyond one day. In case of necessity, however, the next day too. If he stays three days, he is a false prophet. 6. On departing, an apostle must not accept anything save sufficient food to carry him till his next lodging. If he asks for money, he is a false prophet. 7. While a prophet is making ecstatic utterances, you must not test or examine him. For "every sin will be forgiven," but this sin "will not be forgiven" [Matt 12:31]. 8. However, not everybody making ecstatic utterances is a prophet, but only if he behaves like the Lord. It is by their conduct that the false prophet and the [true] prophet can be distinguished. 9. For instance, if a prophet marks out a table in the Spirit, he must not eat from it. If he does, he is a false prophet. 10. Again, every prophet who teaches the truth but fails to practice what he preaches is a false prophet. 11. But every attested and genuine prophet who acts with a view to symbolizing the mystery of the Church, and does not teach you to do all he does, must not be judged by you. His judgment rests with God. For the ancient prophets too acted in this way. 12. But if someone says in the Spirit, "Give me money, or something else," you must not heed him. However, if he tells you to give for others in need, no one must condemn him.

12. Everyone "who comes" to you "in the name of the Lord" [Matt 21:9] must be welcomed. Afterward, when you have tested him, you will find out about him, for you have insight into right and wrong. 2. If it is a traveler who arrives, help him all you can. But he must not stay with you more than two days, or, if necessary, three. 3. If he wants to settle

[9]Text: SC 248. 182-184. ed. by W. Rordorf and A. Tuilier (1978). Trans.: *Early Christian Fathers,* by Cyril C. Richardson (Philadelphia, 1953). 176-178.

with you and is an artisan, he must work for his living. 4. If, however, he has no trade, use your judgment in taking steps for him to live with you as a Christian without being idle. 5. If he refuses to do this, he is trading on Christ. You must be on your guard against such people.

13. Every genuine prophet who wants to settle with you "has a right to his support." 2. Similarly, a genuine teacher himself, just like a "workman, has right to his support" [Matt 10:10]. 3. Hence take all the first fruits of vintage and harvest, and of cattle and sheep, and give these first fruits to the prophets. For they are your high priests. 4. If, however, you have no prophet, give them to the poor. 5. If you make bread, take the first fruits and give in accordance with the precept. 6. Similarly, when you open a jar of wine or oil, take first fruits and give them to the prophets. 7. Indeed, of money, clothes, and of all your possessions, take such first fruits as you think right, and give in accordance with the precept.

14. On every Lord's Day—his special day—come together and break bread and give thanks, first confessing your sins so that your sacrifice may be pure. 2. Anyone at variance with his neighbor must not join you, until they are reconciled, lest your sacrifice be defiled. 3. For it was of this sacrifice that the Lord said, "Always and everywhere offer me a pure sacrifice; for I am a great King, says the Lord, and my name is marveled at by the nations" [Mal 1:11, 14].

15. You must, then, elect for yourselves bishops and deacons who are a credit to the Lord, men who are gentle, generous, faithful, and well tried. For their ministry to you is identical with that of the prophets and teachers. 2. You must not, therefore, despise them, for along with the prophets and teachers they enjoy a place of honor among you. 3. Furthermore, do not reprove each other angrily, but quietly, as you find it in the gospel. Moreover, if anyone has wronged his neighbor, nobody must speak to him, and he must not hear a word from you, until he repents. 4. Say your prayers, give your charity, and do everything just as you find it in the gospel of our Lord.

4. Justin Martyr

FIRST APOLOGY, 65-67

[Tr. by Edward Rochie Hardy]

Justin was a native of Palestine who was converted to Christianity in the course of his search for the true philosophy. He eventually opened a school in Rome, where he taught Christianity, and in 165 died there as a martyr. He had written, ca. 150 or 155, a defense of Christianity, now called the *First Apology*, in which he gives a valuable exposition of Christianity as he understood it, which includes an extended description of the Sunday Eucharist. The text shows the role of the "president" (*proestōs* in Greek), deacons, and a reader. The president has several functions: praying over the gifts, preaching, and overseeing the care of the needy.

65.[10] We, however, after thus washing the one who has been convinced and signified his assent, lead him to those who are called brethren, where they are assembled. They then earnestly offer common prayers for themselves and the one who has been illuminated and all others everywhere, that we may be made worthy, having learned the truth, to be found in deed good citizens and keepers of what is commanded, so that we may be saved with eternal salvation. On finishing the prayers we greet each other with a kiss. Then bread and a cup of water and mixed wine are brought to the president of the brethren and he, taking them, sends up praise and glory to the Father of the universe through the name of the Son and of the Holy Spirit, and offers thanksgiving at some length that we have been deemed worthy to receive these things from him. When he has finished the prayers and the thanksgiving, the whole congregation present assents, saying, "Amen." "Amen" in the Hebrew language means, "So be it." When the president has given thanks and the whole congregation has assented, those

[10]Text: PG 6.428-432. Trans. *Early Christian Fathers*, by Edward Rochie Hardy, ed. by Cyril C. Richardson (Philadelphia, 1953), 285-288.

whom we call deacons give to each of those present a portion of the consecrated bread and wine and water, and they take it to the absent.

66. This food we call Eucharist, of which no one is allowed to partake except one who believes that the things we teach are true, and has received the washing for forgiveness of sins and for rebirth, and who lives as Christ handed down to us. For we do not receive these things as common bread or common drink; but as Jesus Christ our Savior being incarnate by God's word took flesh and blood for our salvation, so also we have been taught that the food consecrated by the word of prayer which comes from him, from which our flesh and blood are nourished by transformation, is the flesh and blood of that incarnate Jesus. For the apostles in the memoirs composed by them, which are called Gospels, thus handed down what was commanded them: that Jesus, taking bread and having given thanks, said, "Do this for my memorial, this is my body" [1 Cor 11:24; Luke 22:19]; and likewise taking the cup and giving thanks he said, "This is my blood" [Matt 26:28]; and gave it to them alone. This also the wicked demons in imitation handed down as something to be done in the mysteries of Mithra; for bread and a cup of water are brought out in their secret rites of initiation, with certain invocations which you either know or can learn.

67. After these services we constantly remind each other of these things. Those who have more come to the aid of those who lack, and we are constantly together. Over all that we receive we bless the Maker of all things through his Son Jesus Christ and through the Holy Spirit. And on the day called Sunday there is a meeting in one place of those who live in cities or the country, and the memoirs of the apostles or the writings of the prophets are read as long as time permits. When the reader has finished, the president in a discourse urges and invites us to the imitation of these noble things. Then we all stand up together and offer prayers. And, as said before, when we have finished the prayer, bread is brought, and wine and water, and the president similarly sends up prayers and thanksgivings to the best of his ability, and the congregation assents, saying the Amen; the distribution, and reception of the consecrated elements by each one, takes place and they are sent to the absent by the deacons. Those who prosper, and who so wish, contribute, each one as much as he chooses to. What is collected is deposited with the president, and he takes care of orphans and widows, and those who are in want on account of sickness or any other cause, and those who are in bonds, and the strangers who are sojourners among us, and, briefly, he is the protector of all those in need. We all hold this common gathering on Sunday, since it is the first day, on which God transforming darkness and matter made the universe, and Jesus Christ our Savior rose from the dead on the same day. For they crucified him on the day before Saturday, and, on the day after Saturday, he appeared to his apostles and disciples and taught them these things which I have passed on to you also for your serious consideration.

5. Hippolytus of Rome
Apostolic Tradition (excerpts)

Hippolytus of Rome is a mysterious figure, and little can be said of him with certainty. He may have been born in the East. He was ordained a presbyter at Rome. He wrote extensively, occasionally in opposition to the official church leaders at Rome. He probably died as a martyr in 235. The *Apostolic Tradition*, which he wrote ca. 220, has been reconstructed from ancient fragments and translations. As the prologue indicates, it is a conservative work, an attempt to maintain the traditions of the church in the face of change. It may therefore be a good representation of the liturgy at Rome ca. 200. It contains the oldest extant ordination prayers for bishops, presbyters and deacons, and gives good indications of the development of other offices and functions in the church. The translation is from Botte's French text, which he considered his critical reconstruction of the original.

1.[11] *Prologue*

We have properly explained the part of the discourse which deals with the charisms, that is, all those gifts which God, according to his will, gave to men from the beginning, restoring to them that image which had been lost.

Now, moved by charity toward all the saints, we have come to the essence of the tradition which befits the churches, so that those who are well instructed might preserve the tradition which has endured up to the present time. Following our exposition of the tradition and making themselves familiar with it, they should be strengthened. The reason for this is the fall or error which was recently brought about by ignorance, and because of ignorant people. The Holy Spirit will confer perfect grace on those who have a right faith, so that they will know how those who are at the head of the church should teach and preserve all these matters.

2. Bishops

That man should be ordained a bishop who was chosen by the whole people, and is without reproach. When his name has been brought forth and he is acceptable, the people will assemble on Sunday with the presbytery and the bishops who are present. With the consent of all, the bishops impose hands on him; the presbytery stands by without doing anything. All keep silence, praying in their hearts for the descent of the Spirit. After this, one of the bishops present, at the request of all, while imposing hands on him who is being made bishop, prays and says:

3. Prayer of episcopal ordination

"God and Father of our Lord Jesus Christ, Father of mercies and God of all consolation, who dwell in highest heavens and regard what is humble, who know all things before they exist, who gave laws to your Church by the word of your grace, who predestined the race of the just descen-

[11]Text: SC 11 bis, 38-46, 56-68, 122, ed. by B. Botte (1968).

dants of Abraham from the beginning, who established leaders and priests and did not leave your sanctuary without service: it has pleased you since the foundation of the world to be glorified in those whom you have chosen. Pour out now again the power which comes from you, that of the sovereign Spirit, which you gave to your beloved child Jesus Christ, and which he gave to your holy apostles who founded the Church in every place as your sanctuary, for the glory and unceasing praise of your name.

"Father, knower of hearts, grant that your servant whom you have chosen for the episcopate may pasture your holy flock and exercise the sovereign priesthood before you without reproach, serving you night and day. May he propitiate your face ceaselessly, and offer the gifts of your holy Church. May he have the power to forgive sins, in virtue of the spirit of the sovereign priesthood, according to your commandment. May he distribute the offices according to your order, and loosen every bond in virtue of the power which you gave to the apostles. May he please you by his gentleness and his pure heart, offering you an acceptable fragrance, through your child Jesus Christ, through whom be glory, power, honor to you with the Holy Spirit in the holy Church, now and for ages of ages. Amen."

7. Presbyters

When a presbyter is ordained, let the bishop impose his hand on his head, while the presbyters also touch him. He should speak as above, as we have prescribed for a bishop, praying and saying:

"God and Father of our Lord Jesus Christ, look upon this servant of yours and give him the Spirit of the grace and counsel of the presbyterate, so that he might help and govern your people with a pure heart, just as you showed concern for your chosen people and commanded Moses to choose elders, whom you filled with the Spirit which you gave to your servant. Now again, Lord, give the Spirit of your grace and keep it unfailing in us. Render us worthy, once filled with this Spirit, to serve you in simplicity of heart, praising you through your child Jesus Christ, through whom be glory and power to you, with the Holy Spirit in the holy Church, now and for ages of ages. Amen."

8. Deacons

When a deacon is ordained, he should be chosen as was said above. The bishop alone imposes hands, as we have prescribed. At the ordination of a deacon, the bishop alone should impose hands, because the deacon is not ordained for priesthood, but for the service of the bishop, to do that which the bishop bids him. Indeed he is not a part of the council of the clergy, but he serves, and tells the bishop what is needed. He does not receive the common spirit of the presbytery, which the presbyters share, but that which is entrusted to him under the power of the bishop. That is why the bishop alone ordains the deacon. But for a presbyter, the presbyters also impose hands, because of the common Spirit, as befits their charge. The presbyter, indeed, has only the power to receive it; he does not have the power to give it. Thus he does not ordain clerics. Nevertheless, for the ordination of a presbyter, he makes the gesture while the bishop ordains.

Let the bishop speak thus over the deacon:

"God, who created all and disposed all by the Word, Father of our Lord Jesus Christ, whom you sent to serve according to your will, and to manifest your plan to us, give the Spirit of grace and zeal to your servant, whom you have chosen to serve your Church and to present in your sanctuary that which is offered to you by him who is established as your high priest, to the glory of your name. May he serve you without reproach and in a pure life, and thus obtain a higher rank; may he praise and glorify you through your child Jesus Christ our Lord, through whom be glory, power, praise to you with the Holy Spirit, now and always and for ages of ages. Amen."

9. Confessors

If a confessor was arrested because of the Lord's name, hands will not be imposed on him for the diaconate or the presbyterate, because he possesses the honor of the presbyterate by his confession. But if he is ordained a bishop, hands will be imposed on him.

But if there is a confessor who was not brought before the authorities, or arrested, or sent to prison, or condemned to another punishment, but who at the time was held up to derision for the name of our Lord and punished unofficially, hands should be imposed on him for every order of which he is worthy, if he confessed the faith.

Let the bishop give thanks as we have stated above. When he gives thanks to God, it is not absolutely necessary for him to speak the same words which we have given, as if he were trying to recite them from memory. Let each one pray as he is able. If someone is able to pray for an extended period and to speak a solemn prayer, it is good. But if someone says only a shorter prayer when he prays, he should not be prevented from praying, provided he says a prayer that is sound and orthodox.

10. Widows

When a widow is enrolled, she is not ordained, but designated by this title. If her husband has been dead for a long time, she should be enrolled. But if her husband has died a short time before, she should not be trusted. Even if she is elderly, she should be tested for a certain time, for often the passions live to an old age in one who made a place for them in herself. A widow should be enrolled only by a word; she should join the other widows. Hands will not be imposed on her, because she does not offer the sacrifice and has no liturgical ministry. Ordination is given to clerics because of liturgical ministry. A widow is enrolled for prayer, and this function is common to all.

11. The lector

The lector is enrolled when the bishop gives him the book; he does not receive the imposition of hands.

12. The virgin

Hands are not imposed on a virgin; her decision alone makes her a virgin.

13. The subdeacon

Hands are not imposed on a subdeacon; he is named to follow the deacon.

14. The gifts of healing

If someone says, I have received the gift of healing in a revelation, hands are not imposed on him. The facts themselves will show whether he spoke the truth.

34. That the deacons should be attentive to the bishop

Each deacon, with the subdeacons, will pay careful attention to the bishop. The bishop should be told who are sick, so that, if he wishes, he may visit them. It is a great consolation for a sick person if the high priest is mindful of him.

39. Deacons and presbyters

The deacons and the presbyters will assemble daily in the place which the bishop prescribes for them. The deacons will not fail to be present each time, unless sickness prevents them. When all are assembled, they should teach those who are in the church, and then, after they have prayed, each should go to his proper work.

6. Didascalia apostolorum
Excerpts

[Tr. by R. Hugh Connolly.]

The *Didascalia apostolorum* or *Instruction of the Apostles* is an anonymous work, probably composed in Syria by a bishop in the first half of the third century. Like the *Didache* (only much longer) the *Didascalia* is a church order, giving moral instruction for the faithful and canonical regulations for the constitution of the community. The passages reproduced here give a good idea of how the office of bishop had developed by the early third century. The fourth chapter goes far beyond the pastoral Epistles (which are cited extensively) in describing the qualities requisite in a bishop, even quoting the Old Testament as prescriptive in the matter. Common sense and knowledge of the Bible are also proposed as highly desirable qualities in a bishop. Chapter eight is a moral exhortation addressed directly to bishops. Chapter nine, which has several reminiscences of Ignatius of Antioch, shows how the self-awareness of the clerical state had developed, particularly through the vocabulary of the cultic parts of the Old Testament. The sixteenth chapter is a good account of the necessary roles of deaconesses in the church.

IV. Teaching what manner of man he is that is chosen for the bishopric, and of what sort his conduct should be.

1.[12] But concerning the bishopric, hear ye. The pastor who is appointed bishop and head among the presbytery in the Church in every congregation, "it is required of him that he be blameless, in nothing reproachable" [1 Tim 3:2; Titus 1:7], one remote from all evil, a man not less than fifty years of age, who is now removed from the manners of youth and from the lusts of the Enemy, and from the slander and blasphemy of false brethren, which they bring against many because they understand not that word which is said in the Gospel: "Every one that shall say an idle word, shall give an answer concerning it to the Lord in the day of judgment: for from your words you shall be justified, and from your words you shall be condemned" [Matt 12:36-37]. But if it be possible, let him be instructed and apt to teach; but if he know not letters, let him be versed and skilled in the word, and let him be advanced in years.

2. But if the congregation be a small one, and there be not found a man advanced in years of whom they give testimony that he is wise and suitable to stand in the bishopric: but there be found there one who is young, of whom they that are with him give testimony that he is worthy to stand in the bishopric, and who, though he is young, yet by meekness and quietness of conduct shows maturity: let him be proved

[12]Text of the Verona Latin fragments and translation of the complete Syriac text by R. Hugh Connolly, *Didascalia Apostolorum*, (Oxford, 1929), 29-36.

whether all give testimony concerning him, and so let him sit in peace. For Solomon also at the age of twelve years reigned over Israel; and Josiah at the age of eight years reigned with righteousness; and Joash likewise reigned when seven years old. Wherefore, even though he be young, yet let him be meek and fearful and quiet; for the Lord God said in Isaiah: "On whom shall I look and take pleasure (in him), but on the quiet and meek, that trembles at my words?" [Isa 66:2]. And in the Gospel also He spoke thus: "Blessed are the meek, for they shall inherit the earth" [Matt 5:5]. And let him be merciful; for He said again the Gospel thus: "Blessed are the merciful, for upon them there shall be mercy" [Matt 5:7]. And again let him be a peacemaker; for He says: "Blessed are the peacemakers, for they shall be called the sons of God" [Matt 5:9]. And let him be clear of all evil and wrong and iniquity; for He says again: "Blessed are the pure in heart, for they shall see God" [Matt 5:8]. And let him be "watchful and chaste and staid" [1 Tim 3:2] and orderly; and let him not be turbulent, "and let him not be one that exceeds in wine; and let him not be a backbiter; but let him be quiet, and not be quarrelsome; and let him not be money-loving. And let him not be youthful in mind, lest he be lifted up and fall into the judgment of Satan: for every one that exalts himself shall be humbled" [1 Tim 3:3, 6; Luke 14:11; 18:14]. But it is required that the bishop be thus: "a man that has taken one wife, that has governed his house well" [1 Tim 3:2, 4]. And thus let him be proved when he receives the imposition of hands to sit in the office of the bishopric: whether he be chaste, and whether his wife also be a believer and chaste; and whether he has brought up his children in the fear of God, and admonished and taught them; and whether his household fear and reverence him, and all of them obey him. For if his household in the flesh withstand him and obey him not, how shall they that are without his house become his, and be subject to him?

3. And let him be proved whether he be without blemish in the things of the world, and likewise in his body; for it is written: "See that there be no blemish in him that stands up to be priest" [Lev 21:17]. But let him be also without anger;

for the Lord says: "Anger destroys even the wise" [Prov 15:1]. And let him be merciful and gracious and full of love; for the Lord says: "Love covers a multitude of sins" [1 Pet 4:8]. And let his hand be open to give; and let him love the orphans with the widows, and be a lover of the poor and of strangers. And let him be alert in his ministry, and constant in ministration; and let him be afflicting his soul, and not be one that is put to confusion. And let him know who is the more worthy to receive; for if there be a widow who has somewhat, or is able to nourish herself with that which she needs for her bodily sustenance; and there be another who, though she is not a widow, is in want, whether by reason of sickness, or of the rearing of children, or of bodily infirmity: to this latter rather let him stretch out his hand. But if there be any man who is dissolute, or drunken, or idle, and he be in straits for bodily nourishment, the same is not worthy of an alms, neither of the Church.

4. And let the bishop be also without respect of persons, and let him not defer to the rich nor favor them unduly; and let him not disregard or neglect the poor, nor be lifted up against them. And let him be scant and poor in his food and drink, that he may be able to be watchful in admonishing and correcting those who are undisciplined. And let him not be crafty and extravagant, nor luxurious, nor pleasure-loving, nor fond of dainty meats. And let him not be resentful, but let him be patient in his admonition; and let him be assiduous in his teaching, and constant in reading the divine Scriptures with diligence, that he may interpret and expound the Scriptures fittingly. And let him compare the Law and the Prophets with the Gospel, so that the sayings of the Law and the Prophets may be in accord with the Gospel. But before all let him be a good discriminator between the Law and the Second Legislation, that he may distinguish and show what is the Law of the faithful, and what are the bonds of them that believe not; lest any one of those under your authority take the bonds for the Law, and lay upon himself heavy burdens, and become a son of perdition. Be diligent therefore and attentive to the word, O bishop, so that, if you can, you explain every saying: that with much doctrine you may abundantly nourish and give drink to your people; for it is written in Wisdom: "Be careful of the herb of the field, that you may shear your flock: and gather the grass of summer, that you may have sheep for your clothing: give attention and care to your pasture, that you may have lambs" [Prov 27:25-26].

5. Let not the bishop therefore be "a lover of filthy lucre" [1 Tim 3:8], and especially from the heathen. Let him be suffering a wrong, and not doing a wrong; and let him not love riches. And let him not think ill of any man, nor bear false witness; and let him not be wrathful, nor quarrelsome; and let him not love the presidency; and let him not be double-minded nor double-tongued, nor given to incline his ear to words of slander and murmuring; and let him be no respecter of persons. And let him not love the festivals of the heathen, nor occupy himself with vain error. And let him not be lustful, nor money-loving: for all these things are of the agency of demons.

6. Now all these things let the bishop command and enjoin upon all the people. And let him be wise and lowly; and let him be admonishing and teaching with the doctrine and discipline of God. And let him be of a noble mind, and aloof from all the evil artifices of this world, and from all the evil lust of the heathen. And let his mind be keen to discern, that he may know beforehand them that are evil: and do you keep yourselves from them. But let him be the friend of all, being a righteous judge. And whatever of good there be that is found in men, let the same be in the bishop. For when the pastor shall be remote from all evil, he will be able to constrain his disciples also and encourage them by his good manners to be imitators of his good works; as the Lord has said in the Twelve Prophets: "The people shall be even as the priest" [Hos 4:9]. For it behooves you to be an example to the people, for you also have Christ for an example. Be you therefore also a good example to your people, for the Lord said in Ezekiel: "And the word of the Lord came unto me, saying: Son of man, speak to the sons of your people, and say unto them: When I bring the sword upon a land, let the people of that land take one man from among them and

make him their watchman: and he shall see the sword coming upon the land, and shall blow the trumpet and warn the people; and every one that hears the sound of the trumpet shall give ear. And if he take not warning, and the sword come and take him away, his blood shall be upon his head. Because he heard the sound of the trumpet, and took not warning, his blood shall be upon his head. But he that took warning has delivered his soul. But if the watchman see the sword coming, and blow not the trumpet, and the people be not warned, and the sword come and take away a soul from them: he has been taken away in his sins, and his blood will I require at the hands of the watchman" [Ezek 33:1-6]. Now the sword is the judgment, and the trumpet is the Gospel, but the watchman is the bishop who is set over the Church.

VIII. Warnings to bishops, how they ought to conduct themselves.

1.[13] You shall "not be lovers of wine" [1 Tim 3:3; Titus 1:7], nor drunken; and you shall not be extravagant, nor luxurious, nor spending money improperly. You shall make use of the gifts of God not as alien funds, but as your own, as being appointed good stewards of God, who is ready to require at your hands an account of the discharge of the stewardship entrusted to you. Let that suffice you therefore which is enough for you, food and clothing and whatsoever is necessary. And you shall not make use of the revenues (of the Church) improperly, as alien funds, but with moderation; and you shall not procure pleasure and luxury from the revenues of the Church: "for sufficient for the laborer is his clothing and his food" [Matt 10:10; Luke 10:7]. As good stewards of God, therefore, dispense well, according to the command, those things that are given and accrue to the Church, to orphans and widows and to those who are in distress and to strangers, as knowing that you have God who will require an account at your hands, who delivered

---

[13]Trans.: Connolly, 78-82.

this stewardship unto you. Divide and give therefore to all who are in want.

2. But be you also nourished and live from the revenues of the Church; yet do not devour them by yourselves, but let them that are in want be partakers with you, and you shall be without offense with God. For God upbraids those bishops who greedily and by themselves make use of the revenues of the Church, and make not the poor to be partakers with them, saying thus: "The milk you eat, and with the wool you are clothed" [Ezek 34:3]. For the bishops ought to be nourished from the revenues of the Church, but not to devour them; for it is written: "You shalt not muzzle the ox that treads out the corn" [Deut 25:4; 1 Cor 9:9; 1 Tim 5:18]. As then the ox which works unmuzzled in the threshing floor eats, indeed, but does not consume the whole, so do you also, who work in the threshing floor which is the Church of God, be nourished from the Church, after the manner of the Levites who ministered in the tabernacle of witness, which in all things was a type of the Church: for even by its name it declares this, for the tabernacle "of witness" foreshowed the Church. Now the Levites who ministered therein were nourished from those things which were given as offerings to God by all the people—gifts, and part-offerings, and firstfruits, and tithes, and sacrifices, and offerings, and holocausts—without restraint, they and their wives and their sons and their daughters; because their work was the ministry of the tabernacle alone; and therefore they received no inheritance of land among the children of Israel, because the inheritance of Levi and his tribe was the produce of the people.

3. You also then today, O bishops, are priests to your people, and the Levites who minister to the tabernacle of God, the holy Catholic Church, who stand continually before the Lord God. You then are to your people priests and prophets, and princes and leaders and kings, and mediators between God and His faithful, and receivers of the word, and preachers and proclaimers thereof, and knowers of the Scriptures and of the utterances of God, and witnesses of His will, who bear the sins of all, and are to give

an answer for all. You are they who have heard how the word sternly threatens you if you neglect and preach not God's will, who are in sore peril of destruction if you neglect your people. You again are they to whom is promised from God the great reward which is not falsified nor withheld, and grace unspeakable in great glory, when you shall minister well to the tabernacle of God, His Catholic Church. As then you have undertaken the burden of all, so also ought you to receive from all your people the ministration of food and clothing, and of other things needful. And so again, from these same gifts that are given you by the people which is under your charge, do you nourish the deacons and widows and orphans, and those who are in want, and strangers. For it behooves you, O bishop, as a faithful steward to care for all; for as you bear the sins of all those under your charge, so shall you beyond all men receive more abundant glory of God. For you are an imitator of Christ: and as He took upon Him the sins of us all, so it behooves you also to bear the sins of all those under your charge; for it is written in Isaiah concerning our Savior thus: "We saw him having no splendor nor beauty, but as one whose aspect was marred and dejected beyond that of men; and as a man that suffers, and knows to bear infirmities. For his face was changed: he was despised, and was nothing accounted in our eyes. But he endured our sins, and for our sake did sigh. But we accounted him as one smitten and plagued and brought low. Yet for our sins was he smitten, and was made sick for our iniquities: and by his stripes all we are healed" [Isa 53:2-5]. And again He says: "He bore the sins of many, and for their iniquity was delivered up" [Isa 53:12]. And in David and in all the prophets, and in the Gospel also, our Savior makes intercession for our sins, whereas He is without sin. Therefore, as you have Christ for a pattern, so be you also a pattern to the people under your charge; and as He took upon Him our sins, so do you also take upon you the sins of the people. For you are not to think that the burden of the bishopric is light or easy.

4. Wherefore, as you have taken up the burden of all, so the fruits also which you receive from all the people shall be

yours, for all things of which you have need. And do you nourish well them that are in want, as being to render an account to Him who will require it, who can make no mistake nor be evaded. For as you administer the office of the bishopric, so from the same office of the bishopric ought you to be nourished, as the priests and Levites and ministers who serve before God, according as it is written in the book of Numbers: [there follows Num 18:1-32].

IX. An admonition to the people, that they should honor the bishop.

1.[14] Hear these things then, you laymen also, the elect Church of God. For the former People also was called a church; but you are the Catholic Church, the holy and perfect, "a royal priesthood, a holy multitude, a people for inheritance" [1 Pet 2:9], the great Church, the bride adorned for the Lord God. Those things then which were said beforetime, hear ye also now. Set by part-offerings and tithes and firstfruits to Christ, the true High Priest, and to His ministers, even tithes of salvation to Him the beginning of whose name is the Decade.[15] Hear, you Catholic Church of God, that were delivered from the ten plagues, and did receive the Ten Words, and did learn the Law, and hold the faith, and know the Decade, and believe in the Yod in the beginning of the Name, and are established in the perfection of His glory: instead of the sacrifices which then were, offer now prayers and petitions and thanksgivings. Then were firstfruits and tithes and part-offerings and gifts; but today the oblations which are offered through the bishops to the Lord God. For they are your high priests; but the priests and Levites now are the presbyters and deacons, and the orphans and widows: but the Levite and high priest is the bishop. He is

[14]Trans.: Connolly, 85-88, 92-93.

[15]Jesus' name in Hebrew begins with the letter yod, and in Greek with the letter iota; as numerals, both represent 10. The author takes groups of 10 in the Old Testament as types of Jesus.

minister of the word and mediator; but to you a teacher, and your father after God, who begot you through the water. This is your chief and your leader, and he is your mighty king. He rules in the place of the Almighty: but let him be honored by you as God, for the bishop sits for you in the place of God Almighty. But the deacon stands in the place of Christ; and do you love him. And the deaconess shall be honored by you in the place of the Holy Spirit; and the presbyters shall be to you in the likeness of the Apostles; and orphans and widows shall be reckoned by you in the likeness of the altar. And as it was not lawful for a stranger, that is for one who was not a Levite, to draw near to the altar or to offer aught without the high priest, so you also shall do nothing without the bishop. But if any man do aught without the bishop, he does it in vain, for it shall not be accounted to him for a work; for it is not fitting that any man should do aught apart from the high priest.

2. Do you therefore present your offerings to the bishop, either you yourselves, or through the deacons; and when he has received he will distribute them justly. For the bishop is well acquainted of those who are in distress, and dispenses and gives to each one as is fitting for him; so that one may not receive often in the same day or in the same week, and another receive not even a little. For whom the priest and steward of God knows to be the more in distress, him he succors according as he requires.

5. Do you therefore esteem the bishop as the mouth of God. For if Aaron, because he interpreted to Pharaoh the words which were given through Moses, was called a prophet, as the Lord said to Moses: "Behold, I have given you as a god to Pharaoh; and Aaron your brother shall be to you a prophet" [Exod 7:1]: why then should not you also reckon them as prophets who are for you the mediators of the word, and worship them as God? But for us now, Aaron is the deacon, and Moses is the bishop. Now if Moses was called a god by the Lord, let the bishop also be honored by you as God, and the deacon as a prophet. Wherefore, for the honor of the bishop, make known to him all things that you do, and let them be performed through him. And if you know of one who is in much distress, and the bishop know not of him, do you inform him; and without him do not, to his discredit, anything, lest you bring a reproach upon him as one who neglects the poor. For he who sets abroad an evil report against the bishop, whether by word or by deed, sins against God Almighty. And again, if any man speaks evil of a deacon, whether by word or deed, he offends against Christ. Wherefore in the Law also it is written: "You shall not revile your gods; and you shall not speak evil of a prince of your people" [Exod 22:28]. Now let no man think that the Lord speaks here of idols of stone; but he calls "gods" those who preside over you. Moses also says in the Book of Numbers, when the people had murmured against him and against Aaron: "Not against us do you murmur, but against the Lord God" [Exod 16:8]. And our Savior likewise said: "Every one that rejects you, rejects me, and him that sent me" [Luke 10:16]. For what hope at all is there for him who speaks evil of the bishop, or of the deacon? For if one call a layman "fool," or "raca, he is liable to the assembly" [Matt 5:22], as one of those who rise up against Christ: because that he calls "empty" his brother in whom Christ dwells, who is not empty but fulfilled; or calls him "fool" in whom dwells the Holy Spirit of God, fulfilled with all wisdom: as though he should become a fool by the very Spirit that dwells in him! If then one who should say any of these things to a layman is found to fall under so great condemnation, how much more if he should dare to say aught against the deacon, or against the bishop, through whom the Lord gave you the Holy Spirit, and through whom you have learned the word and have known God, and through whom you have been known of God, and through whom you were sealed, and through whom you become sons of the light, and through whom the Lord in baptism, by the imposition of hand of the bishop, bore witness to each one of you and uttered his holy voice, saying: "You are my son: I this day have begotten you" [Ps 2:7].

XVI. On the appointment of deacons and deaconesses.

1.[16] Wherefore, O bishop, appoint workers of righteousness as helpers who may cooperate with you unto salvation. Those that please you out of all the people you shall choose and appoint as deacons: a man for the performance of the most things that are required, but a woman for the ministry of women. For there are houses whither you cannot send a deacon to the women, on account of the heathen, but may send a deaconess. Also, because in many other matters the office of a woman deacon is required. In the first place, when women go down into the water, those who go down into the water ought to be anointed by a deaconess with the oil of anointing; and where there is no woman at hand, and especially no deaconess, he who baptizes must of necessity anoint her who is being baptized. But where there is a woman, and especially a deaconess, it is not fitting that women should be seen by men: but with the imposition of hand do you anoint the head only. As of old the priests and kings were anointed in Israel, do you in like manner, with the imposition of hand, anoint the head of those who receive baptism, whether of men or or women; and afterwards — whether you yourself baptize, or you command the deacons or presbyters to baptize — let a woman deacon, as we have already said, anoint the women. But let a man pronounce over them the invocation of the divine Names in the water.

2. And when she who is being baptized has come up from the water, let the deaconess receive her, and teach and instruct her how the seal of baptism ought to be kept unbroken in purity and holiness. For this cause we say that the ministry of a woman deacon is especially needful and important. For our Lord and Savior also was ministered unto by women ministers, "Mary Magdalene, and Mary the daughter of James and mother of Jose, and the mother of the sons of Zebedee" [Matt 27:56], with other women beside. And you also have need of the ministry of a deaconess for many things; for a deaconess is required to go into the

---

[16]Trans.: Connolly, 146-150.

houses of the heathen where there are believing women, and to visit those who are sick, and to minister to them in that of which they have need, and to bathe those who have begun to recover from sickness.

3. And let the deacons imitate the bishops in their conversation: nay, let them even be laboring more than he. And let them "not love filthy lucre" [1 Tim 3:8]; but let them be diligent in the ministry. And in proportion to the number of the congregation of the people of the Church, so let the deacons be, that they may be able to take knowledge of each severally and refresh all; so that for the aged women who are infirm, and for brethren and sisters who are in sickness—for every one they may provide the ministry which is proper for him.

4. But let a woman rather be devoted to the ministry of women, and a male deacon to the ministry of men. And let him be ready to obey and to submit himself to the command of the bishop. And let him labor and toil in every place whither he is sent to minister or to speak of some matter to any one. For it behooves each one to know his office and to be diligent in executing it. And be you bishop and deacon of one counsel and of one purpose, and one soul dwelling in two bodies. And know what the ministry is, according as our Lord and Savior said in the Gospel: "Whoso among you desires to be chief, let him be your servant: even as the Son of Man came not to be ministered unto, but to minister, and to give his life a ransom for many" [Matt 20:26-28]. So ought you the deacons also to do, if it fall to you to lay down your life for your brethren in the ministry which is due to them. For neither did our Lord and Savior Himself disdain to be ministering to us, as it is written in Isaiah: "To justify the righteous, who has performed well a service for many" [Isa 53:11]. If then the Lord of heaven and earth "performed a service" for us, and bore and endured everything for us, how much more ought we to do the like for our brethren, that we may imitate Him. For we are imitators of Him, and hold the place of Christ. And again in the Gospel you find it written how our Lord "girded a linen cloth about his loins and cast water into a wash-basin," while we reclined at supper, and drew nigh "and washed the feet of" us all "and wiped them with the cloth" [John 13:4-5]. Now this He did that He might show us an example of charity and brotherly love, that we also should do in like manner one to another. If then our Lord did thus, will you, O deacons, hesitate to do the like for them that are sick and infirm, you who are workmen of the truth, and bear the likeness of Christ? Do you therefore minister with love, and neither murmur nor hesitate; otherwise you will have ministered as it were for men's sake and not for the sake of God, and you will receive your reward according to your ministry in the day of judgment. It is required of you deacons therefore that you visit all who are in need, and inform the bishop of those who are in distress; and you shall be his soul and his mind; and in all things you shall be taking trouble and be obedient to him.

2. THE CHURCH IN THE EASTERN EMPIRE

7. Origen
Homilies on Leviticus

Origen was born ca. 185 in Alexandria, and died in 254 in Palestine or Phoenicia. He was one of the most learned and prolific theologians of the early church, equally well known for text-critical work on the Bible, commentaries on almost every biblical book, and theological treatises. In his exegesis, Origen was a determined allegorist, as the passages below illustrate well. The Homilies on Leviticus were preached to catechumens, probably in Caesarea. In discussing some details of Old Testament cult, Origen interprets them as applicable to all Christians, emphasizing the priesthood of all believers (he twice cites 1 Pet 2:9). In homily 6, he also distinguishes the office of priest in the church from the personal qualities that an ideal priest should have, and criticizes the laxity of some of the clergy of his day. His exegesis is based on the Septuagint, not on the Hebrew text. In homily 6, the Greek word for "breastplate" is *logeion*, which Origen interprets through its root *logos*, which means "reason"; and the words transliterated in modern versions as Urim and Thummim were translated "manifestation" and "truth" in Origen's text. This accounts for some of the stranger interpretations in this homily.

HOMILY 6 (on Lev 7:35—8:13)

1.[1] The reason why the words which are read to us can be understood or not understood is explained briefly by the Apostle, who says that "the veil of the Old Testament" can "be taken" from the eyes of the man "who has been converted to the Lord" [2 Cor 3:14,16]. We conclude that he wanted it known that the less clear these matters are to us, the more imperfect is our conversion to God. And therefore we must struggle with all our strength to free ourselves from the preoccupations of the world and from mundane activities, and even, if it is possible, leave behind us the useless talk of our companions, and devote ourselves to God's word and "meditate on his law day and night" [Ps 1:2], so that our conversion might be wholehearted and we might be able to look upon Moses' unveiled face, especially in the words which have been read now, either about the priestly vestments or about the consecration of the high priest. In these passages some things are stated in such a way as to exclude completely that carnal Israel itself from the historical understanding. And so, in order to explain these passages, we cannot depend upon the strength of human intuition, but upon prayers and petitions poured forth to God. In this task we also need your help, so that God, the Father of the Word, might give us a word "to open our mouth" [Eph 6:19] so that we can contemplate the wonders of his law.

2. The beginning of those words which were read today is this: "This is the anointing of Aaron and the anointing of his sons by the sacrifices of the Lord on the day on which he assigned them to sacrifice to the Lord, just as the Lord ordered, to give them this perpetual right for their offspring, on the day on which he anointed them from among the sons of Israel. This is the law of holocausts, of sin offerings, of

---

[1]Text: GCS 29 (Origenes 6) 358-370, ed. by W.A. Baehrens (1920).

offerings for transgression, of consummation, and of saving sacrifice, just as the Lord commanded Moses on Mount Sinai, on the day on which he ordered the sons of Israel to offer their gifts in the Lord's presence in the desert of Sinai" [Lev 7:35-38].

When the law-giver began by saying, "This is the anointing of Aaron and the anointing of his sons," he did not add what the anointing was, nor did he explain how he anointed; this he does in the following passages. But now, after he has said "This is the anointing of Aaron and his sons," he added nothing about the anointing. Actually, he does this to show that what he mentioned previously, that is, "the little breast of application and the arm of separation" [Lev 7:34] are themselves the anointing of Aaron and his sons, lest we think that they are meant to represent carnal realities; they teach us that even these details are included under the mystery of anointing. Then in what follows he repeats what he had explained earlier and says, "This is the law of holocausts, and of sacrifice, and of sin offering." "This" means what was already explained, and seems to be an *anakephalaiōsis*, that is, a recapitulation, of the mysteries which had been explained more fully in the preceding passages.

After this he adds: "And the Lord spoke to Moses saying, 'Take Aaron and his sons and stoles and the oil of anointing and a calf which is a sin offering and two rams and a basket of unleavened bread; and call together the whole assembly at the entrance of the tent of witness.' And Moses did as the Lord commanded him, and he called together the assembly at the entrance of the tent of witness. And Moses said to the assembly, 'This is the word which the Lord ordered done.' And Moses approached his brother Aaron, and Aaron's sons, and he washed them with water and clothed him with a tunic and girded him with a belt. And he clothed him with an inner tunic and placed a cape on him and girded him with the stuff of the cape and bound him in it. And he placed a breastplate on him and over the breastplate he placed manifestation and truth. And he placed a turban on his head, and above the turban before his face a golden, holy, sanctified plate, as the Lord had commanded Moses" [Lev 8:1-9].

With attentive ears and watchful heart listen to the consecration of the high priest and the priest, because according
to God's promises you are also priests of the Lord: "For you
are a holy people and a priesthood" [1 Pet 2:9]. The text
says: according to the Lord's command Moses took "Aaron
and his sons," and first of all he washes them, then he clothes
them. Consider more carefully the order of what was said:
first he washes, then he clothes. For you cannot be clothed
unless you had previously been washed. "Be washed," therefore, "and be clean, and remove your sins from your souls"
[Isa 1:16]. For unless you have been washed in this way, you
will not be able to put on the Lord Jesus Christ, according to
what the Apostle says: "Put on the Lord Jesus Christ, and
have no concern for the flesh in its lusts" [Rom 13:14]. so let
Moses wash you. Let him wash you, and let him clothe you.
You have heard often how Moses can wash you. For we
have often said that, in the holy Scriptures, Moses stands for
the Law, as is written in the Gospel: "They have Moses and
the prophets; let them hear them" [Luke 16:29]. So it is the
Law of God which washes you; the Law itself washes away
your filth; the Law itself, if you listen to it, washes away the
stains of your sins.

It is Moses—that is, the Law—which consecrates priests.
There cannot be a priest whom the Law did not make a
priest. For there are many priests, but the Law did not wash
them, nor the word of God make them pure, nor the divine
word cleanse them from the filth of their sins. But you, who
long to receive sacred baptism and acquire the grace of the
Spirit, ought first to be cleansed from the Law. Once you
have heard God's word you should first restrain your natural faults and put order into your crude and barbarous
morals. Once you have acquired gentleness and humility,
you can also receive the grace of the Holy Spirit, for the
Lord says so through the prophet: "Upon whom shall I rest,
if not upon one who is humble and silent and reveres my
words"? [Isa 66:2]. If you have not been humble and silent, if
you have not received the divine words with reverence, the
grace of the Holy Spirit cannot dwell in you. The Holy
Spirit flees from a soul which is proud and insolent, and

dissembles. You should first meditate on God's Law so that, if your actions are perhaps unrestrained and your morals disordered, God's Law can improve and correct you.

Do you wish to see that Moses is always with Jesus, that is, the Law with the gospels? Let the Gospel teach you, because, when Jesus had been transfigured into glory, Moses and Elijah appeared together with him in glory, so that you might know that the Law and the prophets and the gospels always come together into one and remain in one glory. Peter too, when he wanted to build three tabernacles for them, is reproved for his ignorance, like one who "did not know what he was saying" [Mark 9:6]. For the Law and the prophets and the Gospel do not have three tents, but only one—that is, the Church.

Therefore Moses first washes the Lord's priest; and, when he has washed him and rendered him clean of all the filth of his sins, he clothes him. But let us consider what these garments are with which Moses clothes his brother Aaron, the first high priest. Perhaps it is possible for you too to be clothed with the same garments and to be a high priest. There is one great high priest, our Lord Jesus Christ; but he is not the high priest of priests, but the High Priest of high priests, not the prince of priests, but the Prince of the princes of priests, just as he is not called the king of the people but the King of kings, and Lord, not of slaves, but the Lord of lords. It can happen that, if you have been washed through Moses and are thus clean, like the one whom the great and famous Moses washed, you might also attain these garments which Moses brings, and those stoles with which he clothed Aaron his brother and Aaron's sons. But for the priestly insignia there is need not only of garments but also of cinctures.

But before we begin to speak to the particular kind of garments, I would like to compare those unfortunate garments with which the first man was clothed after he had sinned, with these holy and true garments. God is said to have done this: "For God made tunics out of skins and clothed Adam and his wife" [Gen 3:21]. Therefore those tunics were made of skins and taken from animals. It was fitting that a sinner should be clothed in tunics made of skins, as it says; they are a sign of the mortality which he received because of his sin, and of his weakness, which resulted from the corruption of the flesh. But if you have really been cleansed of these and purified through God's law, Moses will clothe you with the garment of incorruption, so that "your dishonor may not appear anywhere," and "that this mortality may be absorbed by life" [Exod 20:26; 2 Cor 5:4].

3. Let us see, therefore, by what sort of rite the high priest is installed. We read: "Moses called together the assembly and said to them: 'This is the word which the Lord has commanded' " [Lev 8:5]. Although the Lord gave precepts for establishing the high priest, and the Lord chose him, nevertheless the assembly is also called together. For at the ordination of a priest the presence of the people is also necessary, so that all might know and be sure, because that man is chosen for the priesthood who is more outstanding among the whole people, more learned, holier, more eminent in every virtue. And this is done in the presence of the people lest anyone later have second thoughts, or anyone should remain doubtful. This is what the Apostle commanded for the ordination of a priest when he says, "He should also have a good attestation from those who are outside" [1 Tim 3:7].

But I also see something more in the fact that the text says that "Moses called together the whole assembly"; I think that "to call together the assembly" means to collect all the soul's powers and gather them into one so that, when mention is made of the priestly mysteries, all the powers of the soul should be watchful and intent. In these matters the soul should lack no wisdom, no knowledge, no diligence. The whole multitude of senses, the whole assembly of holy thoughts should be present, so that one might reflect in the sanctuary of his heart and understand what the high priest is, what the anointing is, and what his garments are.

So: he washed him and clothed him. With what sort of garment? "A tunic," we read: "and he girded him with a belt and clothed him again with an ankle-length tunic" or, as we read elsewhere, "an interior tunic" [Lev 8:7]. As I see it, Moses clothes the high priest with two tunics. But what do we do, because Jesus forbade his priests, our apostles, to use two tunics? We had said that Moses and Jesus, that is, the Law and the gospels, are in mutual agreement. Perhaps someone might be able to say that what Jesus commanded—not to have two tunics—does not contradict the Law, but is more perfect than the Law. Thus, the Law forbids homicide, but Jesus also restrains anger; and the Law prohibits adultery, but Jesus also cuts off lust in the heart. Thus the high priest, under the Law, seems to have put on two tunics, but under the Gospel the apostles put on only one. Let this interpretation be accepted, if it seems right.

But I do not restrict the mysteries of the high priest to this narrow interpretation. I think that something more is revealed in this detail: the high priest is he who has knowledge of the Law, understands the reasons behind each mystery and—as I shall briefly explain—knows the law both according to the spirit and according to the letter. Therefore the high priest whom Moses ordained at that time knew that there is a spiritual circumcision. But he also kept the circumcision of the flesh, because an uncircumcised man could not be high priest. Therefore he had two tunics: one of carnal ministry and the other of spiritual understanding. He knew that spiritual sacrifices should be offered to God, but he nevertheless kept offering carnal ones. He could not be the high priest of those people who lived then unless he offered up victims. So it is appropriate that that high priest is said to be clothed with two tunics. But the apostles, who were going to say, "If you are circumcised, Christ will be of no profit to you" [Gal 5:2], and again were going to say, "Let no one judge you in food or in drink, or on the division of a feast day, or on the new moon or the Sabbath: these are a shadow of things to come" [Col 2:16-17], are appropriately forbidden to have two tunics. One is enough for them, the interior tunic. Thereby they can completely repudiate the observances of this sort of law after the letter, and not concern their disciples with "Jewish fables" or "impose on them a yoke which neither they nor their fathers were able to bear"[Titus 1:14; Acts 15:10]. They refuse that tunic of the law which is exterior and seen from outside, for Jesus allows them to have one tunic, and that the interior one.

Moses also places a cape on the high priest. This is a decorated garment which is laid around the shoulders. The shoulders are the signs of works and labor. Therefore he wants the high priest to be distinguished in his works, too; knowledge alone is not enough, because "the one who does and teaches, he will be called great in the kingdom of heaven" [Matt 5:19].

4. We read further: "He girded him with the stuff of the cape" [Lev 8:7]. Now he had already said above that "he girded him with a belt" over the tunic, and now he is girded again with the stuff of the cape. What is that double belt with which he wants the high priest restrained on every side? He should be restrained in word and restrained in deed, ready for everything, having nothing remiss or negligent about him. He should be girded with the virtues of the soul, restrained from corporeal vices; he should not have to fear a fault of mind or of body. He should always use both belts, "in order to be chaste in body and in spirit"[1 Cor 7:34]. It is good that he is girded "with the stuff of the cape." According to his deeds and his works he will use the belt of virtue.

After this, the text says, "He placed upon him the breastplate— the word means 'rational element'—and placed upon the breastplate 'manifestation' and 'truth'; and he placed a turban on his head"[Lev 8:8]. But let us see what "breastplate," which is "rational element," could signify. After his nakedness has been covered and his shame veiled with garments, after he has been fortified with works and strengthened with the double belt, the breastplate—that is, the rational element—is then given to him. The breastplate is a sign of wisdom, because wisdom consists in reason. He shows what the strength of this wisdom and reason is. For "he places manifestation and truth over the breastplate." It is not enough for the high priest to have wisdom and to know the reason for all things, unless he can also manifest to the people what he knows. Therefore "manifestation" is placed over the breastplate, so that he might answer every one who asks him for an explanation with faith and truth. And upon that, truth is placed, so that he will not give out what he could think up with his own intelligence but what truth possesses, nor ever depart from the truth, but that truth should always abide in all his discourse. This is what it means "to place manifestation and truth over the breastplate."

Pity those unhappy people who read these words and spend all their intelligence on the meaning of the material vestment; let them tell us what sort of vestment "manifestation" is, or what sort of clothing "truth" is. If anyone ever saw or heard of garments being named "manifestation" and "truth," let them tell us who the women are who wove them, or in what weaving shop these garments were ever made. But if you wish to hear the truth, it is wisdom which makes garments of this kind. Wisdom wove the manifestation of what was hidden, wisdom wove the truth of all things. Therefore let us pray that we may deserve to receive this wisdom from the Lord, and it will surround us with such garments.

But the very order of things, how holy and wonderful it is, behold! "Breastplate" is not first, and "cape" second, because wisdom is not prior to works, but rather works should first exist, and afterwards wisdom should be sought. And then "manifestation" is not before "breastplate," because we should not teach others before we are educated and rational. But over these "truth" is added, because truth is the highest wisdom. And finally, the prophet keeps this same order when he says, "Sow for yourselves for justice, and reap the fruit of life; light up for yourselves the light of knowledge" [Hos 10:12]. You see how he does not first say "light up for yourselves the light of knowledge," but first "sow for yourselves for justice"; and it is not enough to sow; he says "reap the fruit of life," so that you can thereupon fulfill what follows, "light up for yourselves the light of knowledge." Thus even here the decorated cape is put on and does not suffice, but is held in by the belt. But not even this is enough; he is girded a second time, so that the "breastplate" can finally be put on, and "manifestation"and "truth" can follow afterwards. These are the vestments which the high priest uses; the man who exercises the priesthood should be invested with this kind of apparel.

5. But he has not yet finished, and another ornament is still to be added; he must receive a crown. For this reason he first receives the *cidaris*,[2] which is either some covering or some ornament for the head. And after this the turban is put on him. "Before his face," that is, from the high priest's forehead, "a sanctified gold plate" is hung, on which the name of God is said to be engraved. That ornament for the head, on which God's name is said to be inscribed, is put on him after all the other objects with which the lower parts of his body were decorated. This appears to me to show that knowledge of God as the creator of all is more eminent than that of everything else which can be known or understood either about the world or about the rest of creation. And because he is the "head of all" [1 Cor 11:3], that ornament is placed on his head after everything else; for nothing is added to the high priest's head after this. And so those people, of whom the Apostle says that they do not hold fast to "the head," from which any relationship that is made and joined grows for the increase of God in the spirit" [Col 2:19], are wretched.

But if we have understood well what the priest's insignia are, or how his head is honored above all, as we marvel at the depths of the divine mysteries, we should long not only to know and hear them, but also to fulfill and do them, because "it is not hearers of the law who will be justified before God, but doers" [Rom 2:13]. For you, as we have often said already, can do this too. If you have prepared vestments of this sort for yourself by study and watchfulness; if the word of the Law has washed you and made you clean; if the anointing with chrism and the grace of baptism have perdured unsullied in you; if you were clothed with the double garments of the letter and the spirit; if you were also

---

[2]A Greek and Latin form of the Hebrew *kether*, the headdress of the Persian kings.

twice girded, to be chaste in flesh and spirit; if you are embellished with the cape of works and the breastplate of wisdom; if the turban and the gold plate, which are the fullness of the knowledge of God, crown your head: know that, even if you are unnoticed and ignored by men, you exercise in God's eyes the high priesthood within the temple of your soul. "You are a temple of the living God" if "the spirit of God dwells in you" [2 Cor 6:16; 1 Cor 3:16].

What is said after this about Aaron's consecration and anointing we have already explained in passing.

6. When the text says: "And Moses added Aaron's sons, too, and clothed them with tunics, girded them with belts, and placed turbans on them, as the Lord commanded Moses" [Lev 8:13], we should notice how the lesser priests differ from the greater priesthoods. The lesser priests are not given double garments, or a cape, or the breastplate, or the ornament for the head, except the turban and the belt to gird the tunic. They therefore receive the grace of the priesthood, and they exercise that office, but not like him who is adorned with the cape and the breastplate, who is resplendent with manifestation and truth, who is adorned with the ornament of a gold plate. This leads me to believe that it is one thing for priests to exercise their office, another to be learned and distinguished in all things. For anyone can discharge solemn ministry before the people, but there are few who are distinguished by their morals, learned in doctrine, advanced in wisdom, exactly suited to demonstrate the truth of things, and who expound their knowledge of the faith with the elaborate understanding and brilliant exposition symbolized by the golden plate which embellishes his head. Therefore the name of the priesthood is one, but the dignity, according to the merit of a man's life, or the virtues of his soul, is not uniform. And therefore each priest should examine himself in these points which the divine law sets down as in a mirror, and estimate the level of his merit from there. If he sees himself adorned with all the high-priestly insignia which we explained above, if he is aware that he meets this high standard in knowledge, acts and teaching, then he can be assured that he holds the highest priesthood not only in name but also because he deserves it. If not, he should realize that he holds a lower rank, even though he is nominally in the first rank.

Even this, which a careful reader can notice, should not escape our attention, although I have often been uncertain about it in my own considerations—namely, as I read in Exodus [28:4] the place where commands about the priestly insignia are given, I find that eight kinds are made ready for the high priest; but in the passage at hand only seven are enumerated. So I look for what was omitted. The eighth kind mentioned there is the apron or, as we read elsewhere, the linen trousers. Here among the other vestments there is silence about this one. What shall we say? Will we concede forgetfulness in the words of the Holy Spirit so that, when he narrated everything else for the second time, one kind that was previously mentioned escaped his notice? I do not dare to think this about the sacred words. But let us see whether, since we have said previously that this kind of garment seems to be a symbol of chastity, since it apparently covers the thighs and restrains the reins and the loins; whether, I say, one might perhaps say that these parts of the body were not always restrained in the men who were priests at that time, for they sometimes concerned themselves with the future of their kind and the issue of posterity.

But I would not introduce among the priests of the church an interpretation of this sort, for I see something else suggested in this mystery. Priests and teachers in the church are able to beget children, just as he did who used to say, "My little children, whom I bear again until Christ is formed in you" [Gal 4:19]. And again he says somewhere else, "Although you might have many thousands of teachers in Christ, you do not have many fathers. For I begot you in Christ Jesus through the Gospel" [1 Cor 4:15]. So those teachers of the church, in begetting offspring of this sort, sometimes use this restraint and abstain from begetting, when they find the kind of hearers in whom they know that they will not be able to bring forth fruit. And finally, there is a report in the Acts of the Apostles concerning certain persons: "We were unable to speak God's word in Asia"

[Acts 16:6]; this is to have the garment of chaste restraint put on and to refrain from begetting children, because the hearers were such that the seed would perish in them and no offspring could follow. Thus the priests of the church, when they come upon deaf ears, or realize that their hearers are insincere and hypocritical, put on the "apron" and wear the "drawers," and do not make the seed of God's word perish, because the Lord commands this and says, "Do not throw what is holy to the dogs, nor your pearls before swine, lest perhaps they tread on them with their feet and turn about and tear you apart" [Matt 7:6].

For this reason, if any high priest wants to be so not in name but by merit, he should imitate Moses and Aaron. What is said about them? That "they do not depart from the Lord's tabernacle" [Lev 10:7]. So Moses was unceasingly in the Lord's tabernacle. What was his task? Either to learn something from God or to teach the people. These two are the works of the high priest, either to be taught by God through reading the divine Scriptures and meditating on them often, or to teach the people. But he should teach what he has learned from God, not from his own heart; not from human understanding, but what the Spirit teaches.

There is another work which Moses does. He does not go to battles, he does not fight against enemies. What does he do? He prays; and while he prays, his people are victorious. If "he relaxes and lets down his hands" [Exod 17:11] his people are conquered and put to flight. Therefore let the priest of the church pray without ceasing, so that the people who are under him may conquer the invisible enemy, the Amalekites, who are the demons who attack those who wish to live devoutly in Christ. And therefore, meditating on this and recalling it to memory day and night, and being persistent in prayer and watchful, let us beg the Lord to deign to reveal to us an understanding of these things which we read, namely how to observe the spiritual law not only in our understanding but also in our actions, so that, enlightened by the law of the Holy Spirit, we may deserve to obtain the spiritual grace in Christ Jesus our Lord, to whom is glory and power for ages of ages. Amen.

HOMILY 9, 9 (on Lev 16:12)

The[3] high priest, therefore, "takes a shovel filled with burning coals from the altar which stands for the Lord, and fills his hand with mixed ground incense, and brings them into the interior behind the veil" [Lev 16:12]. We should understand first what the narrative means; and then we may ask what the spiritual sense is.

The tent of witness or the Lord's temple is a double building. The first is the one in which the altar of holocausts is located. There is always a fire on that altar. In this building only priests may officiate and celebrate the rites and services of the sacrifices. Access is not granted to the Levites, or to any one else either. The second building is inside and separated from the first only by a veil. Behind this veil are located the ark of the covenant, the mercy-seat upon which two cherubim have been placed, and the altar of incense. Once a year the first high priest, whoever he was, entered this building, after he had offered the propitiatory sacrifices which we explained earlier. He had both hands full, one with a shovel of coals and the other with mixed incense so that once he had entered he could immediately place incense on the coals and smoke would arise and fill the whole building. The cloud of incense would veil the view of the holy things which the high priest's entrance had laid bare.

If the ancient custom of sacrifices is clear to you, let us see what these words contain according to their mystical meaning. You heard that there are two buildings. One of them was visible and open to the priests; the other was, as it were, invisible and could not be entered. The one single exception was the high priest; the others are outside. That first building, I think, can be understood as the church in which we are now, when we are in the flesh. In this church the priests serve at the altar of holocausts and kindle that fire of which Jesus said, "I came to cast fire on the earth, and how much I want it to be kindled!" [Luke 12:49]. And I do not want you to

[3]Text: GCS 29.435-438.

wonder because this building is open only to priests. For all those who are anointed with the salve of sacred chrism are made priests, as Peter says to the whole church: "But you are a chosen, royal, priestly race, a holy people" [1 Pet 2:9]. Therefore you are a priestly race and thus have access to the holy places. Each one of us has in himself his holocaust, and he himself places fire on the altar of his holocaust to keep it burning always. If I renounce everything that I possess and take up my cross and follow Christ, I have offered a holocaust on God's altar. If "I hand over my body to burn, and have charity" [1 Cor 13:3], and obtain the glory of martyrdom, I have offered myself as a holocaust on God's altar. If I love my brethren, so that "I lay down my life for my brethren," if "I struggle for justice and for truth to the death" [1 John 3:16; Sir 4:28], I have offered a holocaust on God's altar. If I make my body dead to all desires of the flesh, if "the world is crucified to me and I to the world" [Gal 6:14] I have offered a holocaust on God's altar and I become the priest of my own offering. In this way, therefore, priesthood is exercised in the first building, and victims are offered.

The high priest is clothed with sanctified vestments, goes out from this building and goes to the inner part behind the veil. We already said this in Paul's words, who says: "Jesus entered not into holy places made by hands, but into heaven itself and appears before God's face on our behalf" [Heb 9:24]. It is therefore the place of heaven, and God's very throne, that is meant by the figure and image of the interior building. But consider the wonderful order of the mysteries. The high priest enters into the holy of holies carrying fire from this altar with him, and takes incense from the exterior building. The vestments too, which he is wearing, he has taken from there. Do you think that my Lord, the true High Priest, will deign to receive from me some part of the mixed ground incense to bring with him to the Father? Do you think that he finds in me some little spark of fire, and my holocaust burning, and will wish to fill his shovel of coals from it, and with those coals to offer the odor of sweetness to God the Father? Blessed is he, the coals of whose holocaust the Lord will find so lively and flaming that he will consider them fit to be put on the altar of incense. Blessed is he in whose heart he will find such a refined and polished and spiritual sense that is so well compounded with the sweetness of different virtues that the Lord will deign to fill his hand with it and offer to God the Father the sweet odor of his understanding. On the contrary, unhappy the soul, the fire of whose faith is extinguished, and the warmth of whose charity grows cold. When our heavenly high priest comes to it and seeks hot burning coals from it, on which to offer incense to the Father, he finds dry cinders and cold ashes in it. Such are all who withdraw and distance themselves from God's word lest they hear the divine words and be ignited with faith, grow warm with charity, and flare up with mercy.

Do you want me to show you how fire goes forth from the Holy Spirit's words and enkindles the hearts of believers? Listen to David speaking in the psalm: "The Lord's words set him on fire" [Ps 119:140]. And again in the gospel it is written, after the Lord spoke to Cleopas, "Were not our hearts burning within us when he explained the Scriptures to us?" [Luke 24:32]. And you—whence will you catch fire? Whence will be found in you the coals of fire, if you are never ignited by the Lord's words, never inflamed with the Holy Spirit's speech? Listen to David himself, who says somewhere else, "My heart grew warm within me, and in my contemplation a fire blazes up" [Ps 39:3]. Whence do you grow warm? Whence is a fire lit in you, if you never contemplate the divine words—or rather, what is even worse, if you grow warm at the circus shows or at the horse races or at athletes' contests? That fire does not come from the Lord's altar. It is the one called "foreign fire," and you just heard a few moments ago that, because some people brought "foreign fire before the Lord, they have been snuffed out" [Lev 16:1]. You grow warm; and when anger fills you and rage blazes up in you, you burn with carnal love and you are tossed about by the fires of the foulest lust. But all of that is "foreign fire" and opposed to God; whoever lights this fire will, without a doubt, suffer the fate of Nadab and Abihu.

8. Gregory of Nazianzus
Oration 2(On His Flight), 95-102

Gregory of Nazianzus (329 or 330—ca. 390) was the son of a bishop, also named Gregory, of Nazianzus in Cappadocia (central Asia Minor). He received an excellent education in rhetoric and philosophy, and became a life-long friend of the bishop Basil of Caesarea. Basil ordained Gregory bishop of Sasima, but he never visited the city. For a brief period in 381 he was bishop of Constantinople, but had to resign. He spent the last decade of his life in seclusion. The occasion of the oration "On His Flight" was his ordination as a presbyter in 362. His father ordained him against his will, and Gregory soon fled to the nearby desert. Upon his return to Nazianzus to assist his father, he wrote an apology for his flight. The passage which follows gives his exalted vision of the preparation necessary for the pastoral office.

95.[4] I know this, and I know that no one is worthy of Christ, the victim and high priest of the great God, unless he has first offered himself to God as a living and holy sacrifice, shown forth spiritual and acceptable worship, and offered to God the sacrifice of praise and a contrite spirit, which is the only sacrifice which the Giver of all things asks of us. How could I dare to offer him the exterior sacrifice which is the image of the great mysteries, or dare to assume the office and name of priest, before consecrating my hands with holy works; before accustoming my eyes to contemplate creation in a wholesome way—that is, only to marvel at the Creator, not to injure the creature; before sufficiently opening my ears to the Lord's instruction, and being given an ear closed to harsh words, but receiving that golden earring with a precious jewel which is the word of a wise man to an attentive ear; before my mouth, lips and tongue were opened to drink in the spirit, were opened wide and filled with the spirit of teaching mysteries and dogmas; before my

[4]Text: SC 247.212-220, ed. by Jean Bernardi (1978).

lips were bound to proclaim in wisdom the fruits of godly perception and also loosed in due season; before my tongue was filled with joy and became the instrument that plays a divine melody roused up by glory, awakened together with the dawn and singing until it cleaved to the roof of the mouth; before my feet stood upon rock, as secure as the stags', and my steps were directed toward God and did not deviate, whether little or much; before every member became an instrument of justice and laid aside all spiritual death which this life has drunk down and which retreats from the spirit?

96. Who will take this risk whose heart has not yet been burned, as the Scriptures were explained to him, by words of God, holy and tested by fire; or has not written out the Scriptures three times on the tablet of his heart, so that he has the mind of Christ; or come to know intimately the dark and unseen treasures that are hidden from the many, so that he beholds the wealth in them and can make others rich, comparing spiritual things with other spiritual things?

97. Who will take this risk who has not yet contemplated the Lord's delight as it should be contemplated, and looked upon his temple—or rather become the temple of the living God, and the living abode of Christ in the spirit? Who will take this risk who has not yet discovered the similarity and distinction of types and truth, withdrawn from the types and submitted to the truth, so that he can escape from the oldness of the letter, and serve the newness of the spirit, and pass wholly over to grace from the law that is fulfilled spiritually in the abolition of the body?

98. Who will take this risk who has not yet made his way through all of Christ's names and powers, in deed and in contemplation, those more exalted and in first place, as well as those that for our sake are humbler and in last place: God, Son, image, Word, wisdom, truth, light, life, power, breath, emanation, reflection, creator, king, head, law, way, door, foundation, rock, pearl, peace, justice, sanctification, redemption, man, slave, shepherd, lamb, high priest, sacrifice, firstborn before creation, firstborn from the dead, resurrection? Who will take this risk who can hear these

names and these deeds heedlessly and does not yet have
fellowship with the Word or partake of him according to the
reality and meaning of each of these titles?

99. Who will take this risk who has not yet dedicated
himself to learning to utter "God's wisdom hidden in a
mystery" [1 Cor 2:7], and is still a child, still being fed on
milk, still one of those not numbered in Israel or enrolled in
God's army; not yet able, like a man, to lift up Christ's cross,
perhaps not yet one of the more honorable members of
Christ? Will he still accept joyfully and eagerly a place as the
head of Christ's fullness? Not if I were the judge or counsel-
or. But this is the greatest of fears, this is the final danger to
every man who perceives the greatness of success, and the
ruin which follows upon failure.

100. Let another set sail to trade, I said; let another be
carried across the wide seas, do battle constantly with the
winds and the waves to gain great profits—perhaps—and to
be exposed to danger, if he is such a good sailor and so
skilled in commerce. I prefer to remain on land, cutting a
short and pleasant furrow, greeting both profits and the sea
from afar, so that I can live thus on a few small barley loaves
and lead a safe life away from the waves, rather than risking
a great and serious danger for great profits.

101. To an exalted man there is a penalty for not under-
taking greater things or extending his power over more
people, but rather remaining content with small things; it is
like lighting a small house with a large lamp, or covering a
child's body with a man's full armor. For a small man,
personal safety lies in carrying a small burden and not
subjecting himself to things beyond his ability, thereby
bringing ridicule upon himself and at the same time running
the added risk, as we have heard, of building a tower that is
suitable for no one else than him who has the means to
complete it.

102. You have the explanation for my flight. Perhaps it is
disproportionate. This is what drove me from you, friends
and brethren; my flight was painful to me and perhaps to
you, but necessary, or it then seemed to me. My yearning for
you, and my perception of your yearning for me, drew me

back. For nothing is so strong in love as the experience of love returned.

9. John Chrysostom
On the Priesthood (excerpts)

[Tr. by Graham Neville]

John, who since the sixth century has been called Chrysostom or golden-mouthed, was born in Antioch between 344 and 354. After a good education he was baptized, and took up the life of an ascetic. In 386 he was ordained a presbyter at Antioch, and until 397 was one of the principal preachers in that church. In that year he was made patriarch of Constantinople on the emperor's demand. His unbending adherence to his own high principles made him unpopular in some quarters; he was eventually exiled and died in 407. The work *On the Priesthood* was composed in 386. It is an imagined dialogue between John and his otherwise unknown friend Basil. John had tricked Basil into accepting ordination as a bishop by pretending that he too would let himself be ordained; the work is an apology for this deceit, and a panegyric of the priesthood (by which Chrysostom means the episcopate). Four selections from this work follow. The first one, and the fourth, show Chrysostom's high estimate of the priesthood. The second portrays the many abuses that might accompany an episcopal ordination. The third is an unusually rich and full treatment of the office of preaching.

III, 4.175.[5] The work of the priesthood is done on earth, but it is ranked among heavenly ordinances. And this is only right, for no man, no angel, no archangel, no other created power, but the Paraclete himself ordained this succession,

---

[5]Text: SC 272. 142-154, 188-198, 280-304, 314-320, ed. by A.-M. Malingrey (1980). Trans.: *Six Books on the Priesthood*, by Graham Neville (London, 1964), 70-74, 89-93, 127-135, 139-142.

and persuaded men, while still remaining in the flesh, to represent the ministry of angels. The priest, therefore, must be as pure as if he were standing in heaven itself, in the midst of those powers.

176. The symbols which existed before the ministry of grace were fearful and awe-inspiring: for example, the bells, the pomegranates, the stones on the breastplate, the stones on the ephod, the miter, the diadem, the long robe, the golden crown, the Holy of Holies, the deep silence within. But if you consider the ministry of grace, you will find that those fearful and awe-inspiring symbols are only trivial. The statement about the Law is true here also: "The splendor that once was is now no splendor at all; it is outshone by a splendor greater still" [2 Cor 3:10]. **177.** When you see the Lord sacrificed and lying before you, and the High Priest standing over the sacrifice and praying, and all who partake being tinctured with that precious blood, can you think that you are still among men and still standing on earth? Are you not at once transported to heaven, and, having driven out of your soul every carnal thought, do you not with soul naked and mind pure look round upon heavenly things? Oh, the wonder of it! Oh, the loving-kindness of God to men! He who sits above with the Father is at that moment held in our hands, and gives himself to those who wish to clasp and embrace him—which they do, all of them, with their eyes. Do you think this could be despised? or that it is the kind of thing anyone can be superior about?

178. Would you like to be shown the excellence of this sacred office by another miracle? Imagine in your mind's eye, if you will, Elijah and the vast crowd standing around him and the sacrifice lying upon the stone altar. All the rest are still, hushed in deep silence. The prophet alone is praying. Suddenly fire falls from the skies on to the offering. It is marvellous; it is charged with bewilderment. Turn, then, from that scene to our present rites, **179.** and you will see not only marvellous things, but things that transcend all terror. The priest stands bringing down, not fire, but the Holy Spirit. And he offers prayer at length, not that some flame lit from above may consume the offerings, but that grace may fall on the sacrifice through that prayer, set alight the souls of all, and make them appear brighter than silver refined in the fire. **180.** Can anyone, not quite mad and deranged, despise this most awe-inspiring rite? Do you not know that no human soul could ever have stood that sacrificial fire, but all would have been utterly annihilated, except for the powerful help of God's grace?

5.181. Anyone who considers how much it means to be able, in his humanity, still entangled in flesh and blood, to approach that blessed and immaculate Being, will see clearly how great is the honor which the grace of the Spirit has bestowed on priests. It is through them that this work is performed, and other work no less than this in its bearing upon our dignity and our salvation.

182. For earth's inhabitants, having their life in this world, have been entrusted with the stewardship of heavenly things, and have received an authority which God has not given to angels or archangels. Not to them was it said, "What things soever you shall bind on earth shall be bound also in heaven; and what things soever you shall loose, shall be loosed" [Matt 18:18]. **183.** Those who are lords on earth have indeed the power to bind, but only men's bodies. But this binding touches the very soul and reaches through heaven. What priests do on earth, God ratifies above. The Master confirms the decisions of his slaves. **184.** Indeed he has given them nothing less than the whole authority of heaven. For he says, "Whose soever sins you forgive, they are forgiven, and whose soever sins you retain, they are retained" [John 20:23]. What authority could be greater than that? "The Father has given all judgment unto the Son" [John 5:22]. But I see that the Son has placed it all in their hands. For they have been raised to this prerogative, as though they were already translated to heaven and had transcended human nature and were freed from our passions.

185. Again, if a king confers on one of his subjects the right to imprison and release again at will, that man is the envy and admiration of all. But although the priest has received from God an authority as much greater than that, as heaven is more precious than earth and souls than bodies, some people think he has received so slight an honor that they can imagine someone entrusted with it actually despising the gift. **186.** God save us from such madness! For it is patently mad to despise this great office without which we cannot attain to salvation or God's good promises.

187. For if a man "cannot enter into the kingdom of heaven except he be born again of water and the spirit" [John 3:5], and if he that eats not the Lord's flesh and drinks not his blood is cast out of everlasting life, and all these things can happen through no other agency except their sacred hands (the priests', I mean), how can anyone, without their help, escape the fire of Gehenna or win his appointed crown? **188.** They are the ones—they and no others—who are in charge of spiritual travail and responsible for the birth that comes through baptism. Through them we put on Christ and are united with the Son of God and become limbs obedient to that blessed Head. **189.** So they should properly be not only more feared than rulers and kings, but more honored even than fathers. For our fathers begot us "of blood and the will of the flesh" [John 1:13]; but they are responsible for our birth from God, that blessed second birth, our true emancipation, the adoption according to grace.

6.190. The priests of the Jews had authority to cure leprosy of the body, or rather, not to cure it, but only to certify the cure. And you know what rivalry there used to be for the priesthood then. But our priests have received authority not over leprosy of the body but over uncleanness of the soul, and not just to certify its cure, but actually to cure it. **191.** So people who look down on them are far more execrable than Dathan and his company and deserve more punishment. For although they claimed an office which did not belong to them, at least they had a marvellous opinion of it, as they showed by wanting it so much. But the people we are considering have done just the opposite at a time when the priesthood has been so embellished and enhanced. Their presumption, therefore, is far greater. **192.** In the assessment of contempt there is no comparison between coveting an honor which does not belong to you and making light of it. Between one and the other there is all the difference between admiration and disdain. **193.** Who could be so beggarly-minded as to make light of these great blessings? No one, I should say, except the victim of some demonic impulse.

194. But, to return to the topic from which I digressed, God has given greater power to priests than to natural parents, not only for punishment, but also for help. The difference between the two is as great as between the present and the future life. **195.** Parents bring us into this life; priests into the life to come. Parents cannot avert bodily death nor drive away the onset of disease; priests have often saved the soul that is sick and at the point of death, by making the punishment milder for some, and preventing others from ever incurring it, not only through instruction and warning, but also through helping them by prayer. **196.** They have authority to remit sins, not only when they make us regenerate, but afterwards too. "Is any among you sick? Let him call for the elders of the Church, and let them pray over him, anointing him with oil in the name of the Lord. And the prayer of faith shall save him that is sick, and the Lord shall raise him up, and if he have committed sins, they shall be forgiven him" [Jas 5:14-15]. **197.** Again, natural parents cannot help their sons if they fall foul of the prominent and powerful, but priests have often appeased the anger of God himself, to say nothing of rulers and kings.

198. Will anyone still dare to accuse me of arrogance after this? I think that after what I have said, such reverence must fill the minds of my hearers that they can no longer accuse of conceit and presumption those who avoid this honor, but only those who seek it of their own accord and are determined to get it for themselves.

III, 15.271. Would you like me to show you one more aspect of this contest which is full of innumerable dangers? Come and take a peep at the public festivals, at which it is the custom for most appointments to ecclesiastical office to be made. You will see the priest assailed with as many accusations as there are persons under his rule. **272.** For all who are qualified to bestow the honor are then split into many factions and the synod of presbyters can be seen agreeing neither among themselves nor with the one who has received the episcopal office. Each man stands alone. One chooses this candidate and another that. **273.** The reason is that they do not all concentrate on the one thing they should—spiritual worth. There are other considerations which influence appointment to office. For example, one man says, "Let this man be chosen, because he belongs to a distinguished family"; another says, "Because he possesses a large fortune and would not need supporting out of the Church's revenues"; another, "Because he is a convert from the other side." One man is anxious to promote above the rest a friend, another a relative, another someone who flatters him. No one will look for the best qualified man or apply any spiritual test.

274. I myself, so far from thinking these are worthy grounds for approving priests, should not dare to select a man quickly, even if he showed great piety (though to me it is no small qualification for that office), unless he combined with piety considerable intelligence as well. **275.** For I know many who have kept themselves under discipline all their life and exhausted their bodies with fasting, and who, as long as they were allowed to live alone and attend to their own needs, were acceptable to God and every day made great progress in this philosophy. Yet when they returned to normal society and had to correct the follies of the common people, they either did not begin to cope with so great a responsibility, or else, when compelled to remain at their post, abandoned their former high standards, brought a heavy penalty on themselves and were not of the least use to others.

276. Again, if a man has spent all his life in the lowest order of the ministry and has reached extreme old age, we will not, simply out of respect for his age, promote him to the next order. What if he should still be unsuitable, even after a lifetime? **277.** I do not say this out of disrespect for grey hairs, nor am I laying down a rule that we should entirely exclude from such responsibility those who come from the monastic fraternity. It has turned out that many even from that body have shed luster upon this office. But I am anxious to show that, if neither piety by itself nor old age alone are sufficient to prove a man worthy of the priesthood, the reasons I have mentioned are hardly likely to do so.

278. Other people go on to give reasons which are stranger still. Some are enlisted in the ranks of the clergy to prevent their siding with the enemy, and others because of their bad character, to stop them causing a lot of trouble if they are overlooked! **279.** Could any worse violation of the right take place than that corrupt men, replete with vices, should be courted for the very things for which they ought to be punished, and promoted to priestly dignity for the very things for which they ought to be forbidden to cross the threshold of the Church? **280.** Tell me, do we need to look any further for the cause of God's anger, when we expose the most sacred and awe-inspiring things to defilement by wicked or worthless men? When some men are entrusted with things unsuited to them and others with things quite beyond their powers, they make the Church as unstable as the Euripus.[6]

281. I once used to deride secular rulers because they distributed honors, not on grounds of inherent merit, but of wealth or seniority or worldly rank. But when I heard that this stupidity had swaggered into our own affairs too, I no longer reckoned their action so strange. **282.** For why should we be surprised that worldly people, who love the praise of the mob and do everything for money, should make this mistake, when those who claim to have renounced all these desires are no better? For although they are contending for heavenly rewards, they act as though they had to decide merely about acres of land or something else of the kind. They simply take commonplace men and put them in charge of those things for which the only-begotten Son of

---

[6]A strait between the island of Euboea and the Greek mainland, proverbial for its uncertain currents.

God did not disdain to empty himself of his own glory and to be made man and to receive the form of a servant to be spat upon and buffeted and to die the most shameful death. **283.** And they do not stop at this, but go on to other actions stranger still. They not merely choose the unworthy; they reject those who are suitable. As though it were necessary to undermine the safety of the Church in both ways, or as though the first reason were not enough to kindle the wrath of God, they have added another reason no less serious. For I think it is as bad to keep out the capable as to bring in the useless. And this is done to prevent the flock of Christ from finding comfort or a breathing-space anywhere. **284.** Does not this deserve a hail of thunder-bolts? Does it not deserve some special hell and not just the one we are threatened with? Yet all these evils are suffered and borne patiently by the one who does not desire the death of a sinner, but rather that he should be converted and live. How can we marvel enough at his love for man, or wonder at his mercy? Christians damage Christ's cause more than his enemies and foes. But the good Lord still shows his kindness and calls us to repentance.

285. Glory be to you, O Lord! Glory be to you! What an abyss of love is in you! How great are the riches of your forbearance! Men who through your Name have come to be worthy and respected instead of mean and worthless use that honor against you who gave it, and dare what is forbidden, and insult what is holy, rejecting and excluding the earnest, in order that evil men may have perfect freedom and full security to subvert whatever they desire.

286. If you want to know the reasons for this scandal, you will find they are like those I mentioned before. They have one root and, so to speak one mother: malice. Yet they are not all of one kind, but different. **287.** One man says, "Reject him, because he is young"; another says, "Because he has not learned how to flatter"; another, "Because he has offended so-and-so." Or again, someone says, "Reject him in case so-and-so should be hurt to see his own nominee rejected and this man appointed"; another says, "Reject him because he is good and just"; another, "Because sinners fear him"; and another gives some other such reason. They have ready to hand all the pretexts they require. Even the number of existing clergy is sufficient argument, when they have no better. Or they argue that it is advisable not to promote a man to this honor suddenly, but gently and by degrees. And they can find as many other reasons as they want.

288. But I should like to ask you now what a bishop ought to do when he has to contend with so many winds. How can he stand firm against such great breakers? How can he repel all these attacks? **289.** If he settles the question by honest assessment, all men become enemies and foes to him and to those whom he has chosen. Everything they do is meant to create hostility to him. They stir up feuds daily and heap endless ridicule on those he has chosen, until they either depose them or get their own men in. It is like a captain having pirates sailing with him on board ship and continually plotting hour by hour against him and the sailors and crew. **290.** If, on the other hand, he prefers popularity with them to his own safety and so chooses unsuitable men, he will incur God's enmity in place of theirs. And what could be worse than that? And his relations with them will be more difficult than before, since they will all conspire together and become so much the stronger. When fierce winds meet from contrary quarters, the sea which before was quiet suddenly rages and towers, and destroys those who sail on it; so the calm sea of the Church, when evil men are accepted, is filled with surf and wreckage.

V, 1.449. I have given sufficient proof of the experience needed by the teacher in contending for the truth. I have one thing more to add to this, a cause of untold dangers: or rather, I will not blame the thing itself so much as those who do not know how to use it properly; in itself it conduces to salvation and to many benefits, when it happens to be handled by earnest, good men. And what is it? It is the great toil expended upon sermons delivered publicly to the congregation.

450. In the first place, most of those who are under authority refuse to treat preachers as their instructors. They

rise above the status of disciples and assume that of specta-
tors sitting in judgment on secular speech-making. In their
case the audience is divided, and some side with one speaker
and others side with another. So in church they divide and
become partisans, some of this preacher and some of that,
listening to their words with favor or dislike. **451.** And this is
not the only difficulty; there is another, no less serious. If it
happens that a preacher weaves among his own words a
proportion of other men's flowers, he falls into worse disgrace than a common thief. And often when he has bor-
rowed nothing at all, he suffers on bare suspicion the fate of
a convicted felon. But why mention the work of others? He
is not allowed to repeat his own compositions too soon. **452.**
For most people usually listen to a preacher for pleasure,
not profit, like adjudicators of a play or concert. The power
of eloquence, which we rejected just now, is more requisite
in a church than when professors of rhetoric are made to
contend against each other!

453. Here, too, a man needs a loftiness of mind far beyond
my own littleness of spirit, if he is to correct this disorderly
and unprofitable delight of ordinary people, and to divert
their attention to something more useful, so that church
people will follow and defer to him and not that he will be
governed by their desires. **454.** It is impossible to acquire
this power except by these two qualities: contempt of praise
and the force of eloquence. **2.455.** If either is lacking, the one
left is made useless through divorce from the other. If a
preacher despises praise, yet does not produce the kind of
teaching which is "with grace, seasoned with salt" [Col 4:6],
he is despised by the people and gets no advantage from his
sublimity. And if he manages this side of things perfectly
well, but is a slave to the sound of applause, again an equal
damage threatens both him and the people, because through
his passion for praise he aims to speak more for the pleasure
than the profit of his hearers. **456.** The man who is unaf-
fected by acclamation, yet unskilled in preaching, does not
truckle to the people's pleasure; but no more can he confer
any real benefit upon them, because he has nothing to say.
And equally, the man who is carried away with the desire for

eulogies may have the ability to improve the people, but chooses instead to provide nothing but entertainment. That is the price he pays for thunders of applause.

3.457. The perfect ruler, then, must be strong in both points, to stop one being nullified by the other. When he stands up in the congregation and says things capable of stinging the careless, the good done by what he has said leaks away quickly if he then stumbles and stops and has to blush for want of words. Those who stand rebuked, being nettled by his words and unable to retaliate on him in any other way, jeer at him for his lack of skill, thinking to mask their shame by doing so. **458.** So, like a good charioteer, the preacher should have reached perfection in both these qualities, in order to be able to handle both of them as need requires. For only when he is himself beyond reproach in everyone's eyes will he be able, with all the authority he desires, to punish or pardon all who are in his charge. But until then it will not be easy to do.

459. But this sublimity must not only be displayed in contempt for applause; it must go further, if its benefit is not in turn to be wasted. 4. What else, then, must he despise? **460.** Slander and envy. The right course is neither to show disproportionate fear and anxiety over ill-directed abuse (for the president will have to put up with unfounded criticism), nor simply to ignore it. We should try to extinguish criticisms at once, even if they are false and are levelled at us by quite ordinary people. **461.** For nothing will magnify a good or evil report as much as an undisciplined crowd. Being accustomed to hear and speak uncritically, they give hasty utterance to whatever occurs to them, without any regard for the truth. **462.** So we must not disregard the multitude, but rather nip their evil suspicions in the bud by convincing our accusers, however unreasonable they may be. We should leave nothing untried that might destroy an evil report. But if, when we have done all, our critics will not be convinced, then at last we must resort to contempt. For anyone who goes half-way to meet humiliation by things like this will never be able to achieve anything fine or admirable. For despondency and constant anxieties have a terrible power to numb the soul and reduce it to utter impotence.

463. The priest should treat those whom he rules as a father treats very young children. We are not disturbed by children's insults or blows or tears; nor do we think much of their laughter and approval. And so with these people, we should not be much elated by their praise nor much dejected by their censure, when we get these things from them out of seasons. **464.** This is not easy, my friend, and I think it may be impossible. **465.** I do not know whether anyone has ever succeeded in not enjoying praise. If he enjoys it, he naturally wants to receive it. And if he wants to receive it, he cannot help being pained and distraught at losing it. **466.** People who enjoy being wealthy take it hard when they fall into poverty, and those who are used to luxury cannot bear to live frugally. So, too, men who are in love with applause have their spirits starved not only when they are blamed off-hand, but even when they fail to be constantly praised. Especially is this so when they have been brought up on applause, or when they hear others being praised.

467. What troubles and vexations do you suppose a man endures, if he enters the lists of preaching with this ambition for applause? The sea can never be free from waves; no more can his soul be free from cares and sorrow. **5.468.** For though a man may have great force as a speaker (which you will rarely find), still he is not excused continual effort. For the art of speaking comes, not by nature, but by instruction, and therefore even if a man reaches the acme of perfection in it, still it may forsake him unless he cultivates its force by constant application and exercise. **469.** So the gifted have even harder work than the unskillful. For the penalty for neglect is not the same for both, but varies in proportion to their attainments. **470.** No one would blame the unskillful for turning out nothing remarkable. But gifted speakers are pursued by frequent complaints from all and sundry, unless they continually surpass the expectation which everyone has of them. Besides this, the unskillful can win great praise for small successes, but as for the others, unless their efforts are very startling and stupendous, they not only forfeit all praise, but have a host of carping critics.

471. For the congregation does not sit in judgment on the sermon as much as on the reputation of the preacher, so that when someone excels everyone else at speaking, then he above all needs painstaking care. He is not allowed sometimes not to succeed—the common experience of all the rest of humanity. On the contrary, unless his sermons always match the great expectations formed of him, he will leave the pulpit the victim of countless jeers and complaints. **472.** No one ever takes it into consideration that a fit of depression, pain, anxiety, or in many cases anger, may cloud the clarity of his mind and prevent his productions from coming forth unalloyed; and that in short, being a man, he cannot invariably reach the same standard or always be successful, but will naturally make many mistakes and obviously fall below the standard of his real ability. People are unwilling to allow for any of these factors, as I said, but criticize him as if they were sitting in judgment on an angel. **473.** And anyhow men are so made that they overlook their neighbor's successes, however many or great; yet if a defect comes to light, however commonplace and however long since it last occurred, it is quickly noticed, fastened on at once, and never forgotten. So a trifling and unimportant fault has often curtailed the glory of many fine achievements.

6.474. You see, my dear fellow, that the ablest speaker has all the more need for careful application, and not application only, but greater tolerance than any of those I have so far mentioned. **475.** For plenty of people keep attacking him without rhyme or reason. They hate him without having anything against him except his universal popularity. And he must put up with their acrimonious envy with composure. **476.** For since they do not cover up and hide this accursed hatred which they entertain without reason, they shower him with abuse and complaints and secret slander and open malice. And the soul which begins by feeling pain and annoyance about each of these things cannot avoid being desolated with grief. **477.** For they not only attack him by their own efforts, but they set about doing so through others as well. They often choose someone who has no speaking ability and cry him up with their praises and admire him quite beyond his deserts. Some do this through sheer ignorance and others through ignorance and envy combined, to ruin the good speaker's reputation, not to win admiration for one who does not deserve it.

478. And that high-minded man has to contend, not just against this kind of opponent, but often against the ignorance of a whole community. For it is impossible for a whole congregation to be made up of men of distinction; and it generally happens that the greater part of the Church consists of ignorant people. The rest are perhaps superior to these, but fall short of men of critical ability by a wider margin than the great majority fall short of them. Scarcely one or two present have acquired real discrimination. And so it is inevitable that the more capable speaker receives less applause and sometimes even goes away without any mark of approval. **479.** He must face these ups and downs in a noble spirit, pardoning those whose opinion is due to ignorance, grieving over those who maintain an attitude out of envy, as miserable, pitiable creatures, and letting neither make him think the less of his powers. **480.** For if a painter of first rank who excelled all others in skill, saw the picture he had painted with great care scoffed at by men ignorant of art, he ought not to be dejected or to regard his painting as poor, because of the judgment of the ignorant; just as little should he regard a really poor work as wonderful and charming because the unlearned admired it.

7.481. Let the best craftsman be the judge of his own handiwork too, and let us rate his productions as beautiful or poor when that is the verdict of the mind which contrived them. But as for the erratic and unskilled opinion of outsiders, we should not so much as consider it. **482.** So too the man who has accepted the task of teaching should pay no attention to the commendation of outsiders, any more than he should let them cause him dejection. When he has composed his sermons to please God (and let this alone be his rule and standard of good oratory in sermons, not applause or commendation), then if he should be approved by men too, let him not spurn their praise. But if his hearers do not accord it, let him neither seek it or sorrow for it. **483.** It will be sufficient encouragement for his efforts, and one much better than anything else, if his conscience tells him that he is organizing and regulating his teaching to please God. **8.484.** For in fact, if he has already been overtaken by the desire for unmerited praise, neither his great efforts nor his powers of speech will be any use. His soul, being unable to bear the senseless criticisms of the multitude, grows slack and loses all earnestness about preaching. So a preacher must train himself above all else to despise praise. For without this addition, knowledge of the technique of speaking is not enough to ensure powerful speech.

485. And even if you choose to investigate carefully the type of man who lacks this gift of eloquence, you will find he needs to despise praise just as much as the other type. **486.** For he will inevitably make many mistakes, if he lets himself be dominated by popular opinion. Being incapable of matching popular preachers in point of eloquence, he will not hesitate to plot against them, to envy them, to criticize them idly, and to do a lot of other disgraceful things. He will dare anything, if it costs him his very soul, to bring their reputation down to the level of his own insignificance. **487.** Besides this, he will give up the sweat of hard work, because a kind of numbness has stolen over his spirit. For it is enough to dispirit a man who cannot disdain praise and reduce him to a deep lethargy, when he toils hard but earns all the less approbation. When a farmer labors on poor land and is forced to farm a rocky plot, he soon gives up his toil, unless he is full of enthusiasm for his work, or is driven on by fear of starvation.

488. If those who can preach with great force need such constant practice to preserve their gift, what about someone who has absolutely no reserves in hand, but needs to get preaching practice by actually preaching? How much difficulty and mental turmoil and trouble must he put up with, to be able to build up his resources just a little by a lot of labor! **489.** And if any of his colleagues of inferior rank can excel him in this particular work, he really needs to be divinely inspired to avoid being seized with envy or thrown into dejection. It requires no ordinary character (and certainly not one like mine) but one of steel, for a man who holds a superior position to be excelled by his inferiors and to bear it with dignity. **490.** If the man who outstrips him in reputation is unassuming and very modest, the experience is just tolerable. But if he is impudent and boastful and vainglorious, his superior may as well pray daily to die, so unpleasant will the other man make his life by flouting him to his face and mocking him behind his back, by detracting frequently from his authority and aiming to be everything himself. And his rival will have derived great assurance in all this from the license people grant him to say what he likes, the warm interest of the majority in him, and the affection of those under his charge. **491.** Or do you not know what a passion for oratory has recently infatuated Christians? Do you not know that its exponents are respected above everyone else, not just by outsiders, but by those of the household of faith? **492.** How, then, can anyone endure the deep disgrace of having his sermon received with blank silence and feelings of boredom, and his listeners waiting for the end of the sermon as if it were a relief after fatigue; whereas they listen to someone else's sermon, however long, with eagerness, and are annoyed when he is about to finish and quite exasperated when he decides to say no more?

493. Perhaps this seems to you a trifling, negligible matter, because you have no experience of it. Yet it is enough to kill enthusiasm and paralyze spiritual energy, unless a man dispossesses himself of all human passions and studies to live like the disembodied spirits who are not hounded by envy or vainglory or any other disease of that sort. **494.** If there actually is anyone capable of subduing this elusive, invincible, savage monster (I mean popular esteem) and cutting off its many heads, or rather, preventing their growth altogether, he will be able to repulse all these attacks easily and enjoy a quiet haven of rest. But if he has not shaken himself free of it, he involves his soul in an intricate struggle, in unrelieved turmoil, and in the hurly-burly of desperation and every other passion. **495.** Why should I catalogue all the other troubles, which no one can describe or realize without personal experience?

VI, 4.516. But most of those who are subject to the priest are shackled with worldly cares, and this makes them more sluggish in the discharge of spiritual duties. Therefore the master must sow his seed practically every day, so that through sheer repetition the word of teaching may be held fast by those who hear. For excessive wealth, great power, indolence arising from luxury, and many other things choke the seeds that are sown. Often the thick growth of thorns does not allow what is sown to fall even as far as the surface of the soil. And again, often the very opposite of these—too much distress, the pinch of poverty, continual insults, and other troubles of that sort—abate men's concern for the things of God. And not even a fraction of their sins can be known to the priests. How could it be otherwise, when they do not know the majority even by sight? **517.** Such are the difficulties of their duties towards the people. But if you go into their duty to God, you will find these difficulties as nothing, since so much greater and more painstaking care is required for this. **518.** What sort of man ought someone to be, who is an ambassador for a whole city—no, not just a city: the whole world—and begs God to be merciful to the sins of all men, not only the living, but the departed too? I do not think that even the confidence of a Moses or Elijah is adequate for this great intercession. He approaches God as if he were responsible for the whole world, and himself the father of all men, praying that wars everywhere may end and tumults cease, supplicating for peace and prosperity, and a speedy release from all ills, private or public, that threaten any man. He must so far surpass all those for whom he intercedes in all qualities as one in authority ought properly to surpass those under his charge. **519.** But when he invokes the Holy Spirit and offers that awful sacrifice and keeps on touching the common Master of us all, tell me, where shall we rank him? What purity and what piety shall we demand of him? Consider how spotless should the hands be that administer these things, how holy the tongue that utters these words. Ought anyone to have a purer and holier soul than one who is to welcome this great Spirit? **520.** At that moment angels attend the priest, and the whole dais and the sanctuary are thronged with heavenly powers in honor of Him who lies there.

521. The actual rites which are performed at that moment are enough to demonstrate this. But I have also heard someone relate the following story. An old, venerable man, who was accustomed to see visions, told him that he had been privileged actually to see it. At that very moment he had suddenly seen, to the extent of his ability, a host of angels clad in bright robes, encircling the altar and bowing their heads, as you would see soldiers bow, when standing in the presence of their king. Personally, I believe the story. **522.** And someone else told me, not from hearsay but as one who had been permitted to see and hear it, that when men are about to pass away, if they happen to have received the Mysteries with a pure conscience just before they breathe their last, a bodyguard of angels escorts them away for the sake of what they have received.

523. Are you not yet frightened at bringing a spirit like mine to such solemn consecration and promoting to the priestly dignity the man wearing dirty clothes whom Christ himself expelled from the general company of guests? **524.** The soul of the priest ought to blaze like a light illuminating the world; but my soul has such darkness enveloping it, through my evil conscience, that it is always hiding itself and cannot frankly gaze upon its Master. **525.** Priests are the salt of the earth. But who could readily tolerate my folly and my complete inexperience, except you with your usual excessive regard for me? **526.** A priest must not only be blameless, as befits one chosen for so high a ministry, but also very discreet and widely experienced. He ought to be as much aware of mundane matters as any who live in the midst of them, and yet be more detached from them than the monks who have taken to the mountains.

527. Since he must mix with men who have married and

are bringing up children, keep servants, own great possessions, take part in public life, and hold high office, he must
be many-sided. **528.** I say many-sided—not a charlatan, a
flatterer, or a hypocrite; but absolutely open and frank of
speech, able to condescend to good pupose, when the situation requires, and to be alike kindly or severe. **529.** It is
impossible to treat all his people in one way, any more than
it would be right for the doctors to deal with all their
patients alike or a helmsman to know only one way of
battling with the winds. This ship of ours is beset with
continual storms; and these storms not only attack from
outside, but are engendered within. Great condescension
and great strictness are both needed. **530.** And all these
different methods look to one object: the glory of God and
the edification of the Church.

10. John Chrysostom
Homilies on the New Testament (excerpts)

John Chysostom's life has already been recounted (see
#9 above). In his thirteen years as a preacher at Antioch
and in the first few years as patriarch of Constantinople,
he explained the gospels of Matthew and John, the Acts
of the Apostles (his is the only complete commentary on
Acts from the first millennium), and the Pauline letters in
an extended series of homilies. Chrysostom was trained
in the school of Antioch, which opposed allegory and
stressed the literal sense of Scripture. Of the passages
below, the first (from the Homilies on John) treats the
intrinsic dignity of the priest. The second, from the Homilies on Acts, is a vivid portrayal of the demands made on
the bishop by the community. The third, an excerpt from
the Homilies on 1 Corinthians, illustrates the role of the
clergy in the preparation of catechumens, and also shows
Chrysostom's attitude toward the sacrament of baptism.
The fourth, from the Homilies on 2 Corinthians, is an
unusual passage in which Chrysostom discusses the ways
in which clergy and laity are the same, and insists on the

importance of consulting the laity. The fifth is a short passage from the Homilies on Philippians, and shows Chrysostom trying to explain the variations in the New Testament titles for the ranks of the ministry. The sixth, the passage from a Homily on 1 Thessalonians, illustrates the sometimes difficult social role of the priest, and treats Chrysostom's view of the benefits brought by the ministry. The seventh and last, from a Homily on 1 Timothy, treats of deacons and deaconesses. The Homilies on John, 1 and 2 Corinthians, and 1 Timothy were preached in Antioch, those on Acts, Philippians and 1 Thessalonians in Constantinople.

HOMILY 86 ON JOHN (on John 20:10-23), 4

Let[7] us do all things so as to be able to have the Holy Spirit with us, and let us treat with great honor those entrusted with his power. For the dignity of the priests is great. Scripture says, "Those whose sins you forgive, they are forgiven" [John 20:23]; therefore Paul also said, "Obey your leaders and submit to them" [Heb 13:17], and hold them in high honor.

You are concerned with your own affairs; and if you manage them well, you will be accountable for nothing else. But the priest, even if he orders his own life well, will depart into Gehenna with the wicked if he is not sharply attentive to your life, and indeed to the lives of all those around him. Often enough, when he is not betrayed by his own conduct, he perishes because of yours, if he has not done all his duty well. Since you know how great the danger is, show priests great good will. Paul himself suggested this when he said, "They keep watch over your souls"—and not just that, but "as men who have to give account" [Heb 13:17]. Priests should therefore receive great reverence from you. But if you too join the others in insulting them, your own affairs will not go well. For as long as the helmsman continues in

Text: PG 59.471-474.

good cheer the passengers' possessions will be safe; but if they are abusive toward him and at enmity, and he is distressed, he cannot be as watchful, or keep his skill in mind, and he unwittingly involves them in countless difficulties. Thus too the priest: if he is revered by you, he will be able to treat your concerns well. But if you drive the priests to discouragement, you weaken their hands and make them— along with yourselves—easy victims of the waves, even if they are very high-minded.

Consider what Christ says concerning the Jews: "The Scribes and the Pharisees have sat on the chair of Moses, so do everything which they tell you to do"[Matt 23:2-3]. Now we should not say, "The priests have sat upon the chair of Moses," but "on the chair of Christ," for it is his teaching that they have received. Thus Paul says too, "We are ambassadors for Christ, as if God were making his appeal through us" [2 Cor 5:20].

Do you not see that all men, even persons who are often superior by birth or morals or intelligence to those who judge them, bow down to the pagan rulers? Because of the one who has conferred the authority, they consider none of these qualities, but respect the decree of the emperor, no matter who it is who has received the authority. There is much fear when a man makes an appointment; but when God appoints someone, we despise the one appointed and abuse him, and plague him with countless reproaches and— although we are forbidden to judge our brethren—sharpen our tongues against the priests. And how can this behavior be excused, when we do not see the beam in our own eye but are overly busy with the speck in another's eye? Do you not know that you make your own sentence harsher when you judge thus? And I say this not to give approval to those who exercise the priesthood unworthily, but pitying them greatly and weeping for them. But I do not say that for this reason it is right for them to be condemned by those they govern, especially by the simplest. For even if their morals are completely discredited, you—if you take heed to yourself— will suffer no harm at all in the matters entrusted to them by God.

For if God caused a voice to be emitted by an ass, and bestowed spiritual blessings through a fortune teller, working through a dumb mouth and the unclean tongue of Balaam on behalf of the offending Jews, how much more will he work on your behalf, who are right-minded? Even if the priests are thoroughly evil, God will effect all that he wills, and will send the Holy Spirit. For it is not the pure man that draws down the Spirit because of his own purity, but grace that effects everything. Scripture says, "All is for your sake, whether Paul or Apollos or Cephas" [1 Cor 3:21-22]. For what has been entrusted to the priest is God's alone to give; and however far human wisdom reaches, it is inferior to that grace.

I say this not so that we will conduct our own lives carelessly, but lest, when some of the leaders live carelessly, you who are ruled will not pile up evil on yourselves. And why do I speak only of priests? Neither an angel nor an archangel is able to change anything that has been given by God; Father and Son and Holy Spirit rules all. The priest only lends his tongue, and offers his hand. For it is not right that those who come in faith to the sacraments of our salvation should be harmed by someone else's wickedness.

If we know all of this, we should fear God and hold his priests in honor, paying them every reverence, so that, both for our own good deeds and for the service paid to the priests, we might receive recompense from God, by the grace and loving-kindness of our Lord Jesus Christ, with whom be glory, power and honor to the Father, together with the Holy Spirit now and always and unto ages of ages. Amen.

HOMILY 3 ON ACTS (on Acts 1:12-26), 4-5

[4.][8] But let me say why this matter became something to fight about: because we come to the episcopate not as if to an office and the leadership of the brethren, but as if to

ˣText: PG 60.39-42

honor and repose. For if you knew that the bishop must belong to all, and bear the burdens of all; if you knew that others are pardoned if they are angry, but the bishop never is; if you knew that others are repeatedly excused if they sin, but the bishop is not; then you would not be eager for his office, or run after it. For he is exposed to everyone's tongue and everyone's judgments, both the wise and the stupid. Every day and every night he is tired out by anxiety. He has many who hate him, many who envy him. Do not tell me about those bishops who curry favor at every turn, those who wish to sleep, those who come to their task as if to repose. I do not speak of these, but of those who are concerned with your souls, those who place the salvation of their subjects before their own salvation.

Tell me: if a man has ten children under his hand permanently in his household, he must think of them constantly; the bishop has so many, not under his hand, not in his household, but owing obedience to his proper authority— what sort of man must he be? "But he is honored," someone says. With what sort of honor? Poor men who earn half a drachma a day abuse him in the marketplace. Why does he not muzzle them? Of course! But, you say, that is not the work of a bishop. Again, if he does not provide for all, both the lazy and the industrious, there are countless complaints from every side. No one is afraid of accusing and slandering him. In the case of civil rulers, fear enters in, but not in this case. The fear of God is meaningless to them.

Why speak of the anxiety about preaching and teaching? Or of the discontent about ordinations? Either I am perhaps very weak and miserable and worthless, or this is the way things are. The soul of the priest is no different from a ship that is tossed on the waves. He is lashed from every side: by friends, by enemies, by acquaintances, by strangers. Does not the emperor rule the whole world, the bishop a single city? But the latter's anxieties are much greater, just as a swollen and raging sea differs from river water stirred by the wind. And why? Because in the case of the emperor there are many to help; everything is ordered by law and rule. In the case of the bishop there is nothing like this, nor is there any authority to give commands. If the bishop is emotionally over-wrought, he is thought to listen without discretion; if he is unmoved, then he is cold. These opposites must meet, so that he is neither despised nor hated. Furthermore, business concerns preoccupy him. How many people must he offend, willingly and unwillingly! How many must he strike at, willingly and unwillingly! I do not speak except from my experience and my situation.

I do not think that there are many among the priests who are saved; many more are perishing. The reason is that the office requires a great soul. The priest has many obligations which drive him out of his natural temper, and he needs countless eyes on all sides. Do you not see how many qualities the bishop must have? He must be able to teach, be forbearing, and cleave to the faithful word in doctrine. How much trouble this requires! And he bears the blame for those who offend others. I pass over other matters; but if only one person dies unbaptized, has he not subverted his own salvation? For the loss of one soul entails a penalty such as no words can describe. If the salvation of that soul is worth so much that the Son of God became man and suffered so much, imagine how great a punishment its loss will bring. If anyone perishes by another's hand in the present life, that man deserves to die; how much more in the other life? Do not tell me that the presbyter has sinned, or the deacon; responsibility for all of this rests on the head of those who ordained them.

Let me say something else. It happens that a bishop has inherited immoral men as clergy. He is at a loss to decide what he should do about bygone sins. There are two cliffs to fall from: he must neither dismiss the man unpunished, nor scandalize the others. Must the man first be excommunicated? There is no present reason for that. Dismiss him unpunished? Yes, someone says; the blame lies with the bishop who ordained him. What does this mean? Should the bishop refuse to ordain him again and raise him to a higher rank? But this will make it clear to all that he is immoral. Again the bishop has given scandal, in a different way. But to raise him to a higher rank? That is much worse.

5. If men sought the high priesthood only as a position of authority, no one would accept it quickly. But as it is, we pursue this office as secular offices are sought. We perish in God's sight in order to be glorified and honored in the eyes of men. What gain is there in honor? How has it been proved to be empty? Whenever you desire the priesthood, compare it with Gehenna, compare it with the punishments there, compare it with the untroubled life, compare it with the measure of punishment. If you sin in your own person, you suffer no great punishment; but if you are a priest, you perish. Consider how much Moses endured, how wise he was, how much good he did. And because he committed one single sin, he was severely punished. And this was fair, because this sin entailed injury to the rest of the people. He was punished more severely not because the sin was public, but because it was the sin of a priest. We do not pay the same penalty for public sins as for private ones. The sin is the same, but the penalty is not the same—indeed, not even the sin is the same, for it is not the same thing to sin in a hidden and concealed way, and to sin openly. The bishop cannot sin secretly. It is fortunate if he does not sin and is freed from any charges; he cannot do so if he sins. If he is angry, if he laughs, if he so much as dreams of relaxation, many people mock him, many are scandalized, many impose rules for him, many evoke the memory of his predecessors in order to abuse him. They do this not because they wish to praise those former bishops, but to hurt the present bishop by bringing to mind his fellow-bishops and the presbyters.

War is sweet to the inexperienced, they say. We prefer to say this before standing in battle. After joining battle, many people cannot see us. We are not engaged now in a war on those who oppress the poor, nor do we dare to defend the flock; but like those shepherds in Ezekiel we slay and devour. Who of us shows as much concern for Christ's sheep as Jacob showed for Laban's sheep? Who is able to recount the frost of the night? Don't tell me about all-night vigils and such services. The opposite is the case. Lieutenant governors and local rulers do not enjoy as much honor as a ruler of the church does. If he enters the palace, who walks first

68174

but him? Among women, or in the houses of the great, no one else outranks him. Everything has perished and gone to ruin. I do not say this because I want to shame you, but to restrain your desire. With what sort of conscience have you become ambitious, either by yourself or through another? With what sort of eyes will you look upon the one who cooperated with you? What excuse will you offer? A man who is reluctant and has been forced to accept an office against his will would have some excuse, even if such a man generally lacks a claim to pardon. But he still has some excuse in the matter. Recall what Simon suffered. What does it matter if you don't give money, but bestow flattery instead of money, and make elaborate preparations, and scheme? "May your money perish along with you" [Acts 8:20]. So Peter spoke to Simon, and so will he say to these office-seekers: may your ambition perish along with you, because you wanted to purchase God's gift by human intrigue.

HOMILY 3 ON 1 CORINTHIANS (on 1 Cor 1:10-17), 6

Not[9] only by these words, but by those which follow, Paul checks their excessive passion, when he says: "Christ did not send me to baptize, but to proclaim the Gospel" [1 Cor 1:17]. This was the more laborious part, and required much hardship and an iron soul, and everything depended on it. Therefore Paul took it upon himself.

Why did he baptize, when he was not sent to baptize? He was not fighting against the one who sent him, but did it above and beyond his call. He did not say that he was forbidden to baptize, but that he was not sent for that, but for what was most needed. Preaching the Gospel is the work of one or two men, while baptizing belongs to anyone who has the priesthood. To take a man who has been instructed and converted and baptize him, is for anyone at all. The

---

[9]Text: *Interpretatio omnium epistularum Paulinarum*, ed. by F. Field (Oxford, 1845-62), II, 25-26.

choice of the person who approaches, and God's grace, do all the rest. When unbelievers need instruction, much work and much wisdom are required. In Paul's time there was also danger involved. In the former case the whole task has been done, and the one to be baptized has already been converted; it is no great thing to baptize the convert. In the latter case there is much labor in winning over the will, changing it to a new outlook, rooting up sin, and implanting the truth. He does not state all this outright, nor does he present an argument and say that baptizing is no work, but proclaiming the Gospel is, because he always knows how to be moderate. But in comparison with pagan wisdom he is earnest, and capable of using quite vehement language.

It was not indeed in opposition to the one who sent him that he baptized; it was like the case of the widows, when the apostles said, "It is not right for us to neglect God's word to serve tables" [Act 6:2]. He did serve, not because he was opposed to them but acting beyond his duty. So too here. We now entrust this work of baptizing to the simpler presbyters, but the function of teaching to those who are wiser, for this is where the work and the sweat are. That is why he says, "Consider presbyters who rule well worthy of double honor, especially those who labor in preaching and teaching" [1 Tim 5:17]. Just as instructing wrestlers is the work of a high-minded and wise trainer, whereas placing the crown on the victor's head can be done by someone unable to wrestle—and still the crown makes the victor more glorious: so without him one cannot be saved, yet the one who baptizes does no great thing, but merely affirms a choice that has already been prepared.

HOMILY 18 ON 2 CORINTHIANS (on 2 Cor 8:16-24), 3

The[10] prayer of the churches freed Peter from his chains, and opened Paul's mouth. The vote of the churches also regulates in no accidental way those who come to spiritual

[10]Text: Field III, 197-200.

offices. For this reason he who is going to ordain someone calls at that time for the prayers of the faithful, and they themselves vote their approval and call out the words which the baptized know. (It is not proper to reveal everything to the uninitiated.) These are times when the priest does not differ from his subject: for instance, when one wants to partake of the awe-inspiring mysteries: we are all equally worthy of them. It was not so in the old covenant, when the priest ate some things, and the people others, and the people had no right to partake of what the priest partook of. But it is not so now. One body lies there for all, and one chalice. And in the prayers too one can see how much the people contribute. The prayers over the possessed and those over penitents are offered together by the priest and the people; all recite one prayer, the one which is filled with pity. Again, when we exclude from the sacred precincts those who may not partake of the holy table, another prayer should be offered, and we all prostrate ourselves together, and all stand up together. Then too, whenever we want to receive or give the kiss of peace, we all give the embrace together. Again, during the most awe-inspiring mysteries the priest prays for the people, and the people pray for the priest; for the words "With your spirit" are nothing else but that. The offering of the Eucharist, again, is in common; for it is not the priest alone who gives thanks, but the whole people. He first speaks in their voice, then they add that it is fitting and just to do this. Then the Eucharist begins.

Why are you amazed if the people somehow speak along with the priest, since he sends up those holy hymns along with the very cherubim and the powers above? I have said all of this so that each of the faithful will live soberly, so that we might learn that we are all one body, differing from each other as limb from limb. We should not cast everything upon the priests, but think of ourselves as members of a common body, the whole Church. This gives us greater security, and provides for greater growth in virtue. Hear about the apostles, how they often made the faithful party to their decisions. When they ordained the Seven, they first consulted with the people. And when Peter ordained Matthias, he consulted with all those present at the time, both men and women. Here, there are no conceited rulers, or slavish subjects, but a spiritual rule which looks for advantage in this, that it undertakes more work and more of the anxiety about you, and not in seeking more hónors. The church must live as one household; all should be disposed like one body, just as there is one baptism, one table, one font, one creation, and one Father.

Why, then, are we divided, if so much unites us? Why are we torn asunder? We are again forced to bewail the same things, which I have often lamented. The present state of things is grievous. We are so divided from each other, yet we should imitate the unity of a single body. For thus the greater will be able to profit from the lesser. If Moses learned from his father-in-law something expedient which he himself did not know, this should happen even more in the church. Why was it that the unbeliever perceived something that the spiritual person did not? In order that all the people then alive might learn that he was a man; that even if he divided the sea and split open the rock, he still needed God's grace; and that those were not deeds of human nature, but of God's power. And now, if one man does not say what is necessary, let another stand up and speak. If he is lowly, but makes a good contribution, confirm his opinion. Even if he is one of the lowliest, do not dishonor him. No one of these people is as far from his neighbor as Moses' father-in-law was from him. And Moses did not disdain to hear him, but took his advice, and was persuaded. He made a written record of it, and was not ashamed to hand down the account in his narrative, and thus demolished the pride of many. For this reason he also left this account, writing it as it were on a pillar for the world, for he knew that it would be useful to many people.

Let us not overlook those who give us useful advice, even if it comes from one of the laity, or a lowly person. Nor do we deserve to have whatever we ourselves suggest prevail in every case. Whatever seems profitable should be ratified by all. Many people with weak eyes perceive things better than those with sharp vision, because they are careful and concentrate their ability. Do not say, "Why do you call me to a meeting, if you do not listen to what I say?" This is not the objection of a counselor, but of a tyrant. The counselor has only the right to speak his own opinion. If something else appears more profitable, and he still wishes to enact his own opinion, he is no longer a counselor, but a tyrant, as I said. Let us not act thus, but free our minds of all pride and foolishness. Let us not consider only how to make our own interests prevail, but how the view that is agreed upon might prevail, even if we did not propose it. Even if we have not found the right way, we gain no small advantage if we receive what comes from others. We will receive an abundant reward from God, and thus too will attain glory. For as the one who offers the right course of action is wise, so we shall reap the approval of intelligence and good sense if we accept it. If households, cities, and the church are thus ordered, they will receive a larger increase. If we thus order the present life in the best way, we will receive the good things to come; and may it be that all of us receive them, by the grace and loving-kindness of our Lord Jesus Christ, to whom be glory for ages of ages. Amen.

HOMILY 2 (1) ON PHILIPPIANS (on Phil 1:1-7), 1

"To[11] the saints in Christ Jesus who are in Philippi" [Phil 1:1]. Since it was likely that the Jews also called themselves saints from the first testament, when they were called a holy people, God's own, Paul added "to the saints in Christ Jesus." For only these are holy; the former are now profane. "To fellow bishops and deacons" [ibid.].[12] Why does he say this? Were there many bishops of one city? Hardly. But that is the way he named the presbyters. For a while they had their titles in common, and the bishop was called a deacon. This is why, when he wrote to Timothy, he said, "Fulfill your

[11]Text: Field V, 8.

[12]Chrysostom understands the text this way; the usual translation is "with the bishops and deacons."

diaconate" [2 Tim 4:5], even though he was a bishop. Since he was a bishop, Paul says to him, "Do not lay hands on any one hastily" [1 Tim 5:22], and "What was given to you with the laying on of hands of the presbytery. . ." [1 Tim 4:14]. Yet presbyters would not ordain a bishop. And again, writing to Titus, he says, "For this reason I left you in Crete, that you might establish presbyters in each city, as I instructed you; if any man is blameless, the husband of one wife. . ." [Titus 1:5-6]; and he says that these are the qualifications of a bishop. When he has said this, he adds immediately, "The bishop must be blameless, as God's steward, and not self-willed" [Titus 1:7]. As I said, in former times the presbyters were called bishops and deacons of Christ, and the bishops were called presbyters. For this reason, many bishops even now address their letters to a "fellow presbyter" and "fellow deacon." But otherwise the proper title is assigned to each rank, the bishop and the presbyter. "To fellow bishops," he says, "and deacons, grace to you and peace from God our Father and the Lord Jesus Christ" [Phil 1:1]

HOMILY 10 ON 1 THESSALONIANS (on 1 Thess 5:12-18), 1

A[13] ruler is often forced to provoke dissension. Just as physicians' servants must cause much pain to the sick, as they prepare both food and drugs which give no pleasure but much benefit, and just as fathers are often burdensome to their children, the same is true of teachers—and even more true. For even if the physician is hated by the sick man, he still has the man's relatives and friends well disposed toward himself; and often enough the sick man is, too. And a father exercises dominion over his child with great ease, both because of nature and because of external laws. If he should chastise or rebuke an unwilling child, no one will hinder him, nor will the child be able to oppose him. But in the case of the priest there is much discontent. First of all he

[13]Text: Field V, 420-423.

should be governing willing subjects who are grateful to him for his rule; but it is not possible that this will soon be the case. The one who is reproved and blamed, whatever sort of man he is, will soon lose his gratitude completely, and will be hostile. The man who is given advice, or warned, or exhorted will act in the same way. Therefore if I tell someone, spend your money on the needy, I have said something oppressive and burdensome. If I say, restrain your anger, or quench your wrath, or put an end to your perverse desire, or cut back a small part of your luxury, this is all burdensome and oppressive. And if I chastise someone who is lazy, or remove him from the church, or exclude him from the common prayer, he is distressed, not because he is deprived of these things, but because of the public disgrace. This is the aggravation of the disease: kept from spiritual benefits, we are grieved not because we are deprived of such great goods, but because we are ashamed before those who see us. We have no awe or fear of the failing itself.

For this reason Paul has much to say about such persons throughout his letters. And Christ bound them under so strict a constraint that he says, "The scribes and the Pharisees have sat on Moses' chair. Do everything they tell you to do, but do not act according to their deeds" [Matt 23:2-3]. Again, when he healed the leper he said, "Go, show yourself to the priest, and offer the gift which Moses prescribed as a testimony to them" [Matt 8:4]. And you say, "You make him twice as much a son of Gehenna as yourselves" [Matt 23:15]. This is why I said that he said, "Do not do what they do" [Matt 23:3]. Therefore he has excluded every excuse on the part of a subject. Paul, writing to Timothy, said, "The presbyters that rule well should be deemed worthy of double honor" [1 Tim 5:17]. And, writing to the Hebrews he said, "Obey your superiors and submit to them" [Heb 13:17]; and in the letter we are treating, "We beseech you, brethren, to recognize those who labor among you, and those set over you in the Lord" [1 Thess 5:12]. For when he said, "Build one another up" [1 Thess 5:11], lest they think that he raised them up to the dignity of teachers, he all but added: But observe that I entrusted you with building each other up; for it is not possible for the teacher to say everything. "Those who labor among you, and those set over you in the Lord, and those who admonish you" [1 Thess 5:12], he says. And how is it not absurd, he says, if when a man acts as your protector before a man, you do everything, and pour out your gratitude, but when he acts as your protector before God, you express no gratitude? And, someone says, how does he act as your protector? By praying for you, by administering the spiritual gift which comes through baptism, by visiting, advising and admonishing you. If you call, he comes in the middle of the night. Yet you speak of nothing else but him, and he bears with your nasty language. What sort of constraint did he have? Did he act well, or badly? You have a wife; you live luxuriously; you choose an occupation in business. The priest has devoted himself to this work, and has no other life except being concerned with the church.

Paul says: "Esteem them very highly in love because of their work; be at peace with them" [1 Thess 5:13]. Do you see how he knew of the dissension to come? He does not simply say, "love," but "very highly," as children love their fathers. Through them you were begotten in generation for eternity; through them you have obtained the kingdom. Through their hands all things are done; through them the gates of heaven are opened for you. Let no one rebel, let no one be obstinate. If someone loves Christ, he will also love the priest, no matter what sort of man the priest is, because the awe-inspiring mysteries take place through him. Tell me: if you wanted to see a palace gleaming with abundant gold and flashing with the splendor of jewels, and you found the one who has the keys; and when you asked him, he opened it immediately and admitted you, would you not esteem him above all others? Would you not love him as much as your eyes? Would you not cherish him? The priest opened heaven for you, and you don't cherish him and treat him well? If you have a wife, do you not regard the one who obtained her for you above all others? Thus too, if you love Christ, if you love the kingdom of heaven, acknowledge those through whom you obtained it. This is why Paul says, "Because of their work, be at peace with them" [1 Thess 5:13].

HOMILY 11 ON 1 TIMOTHY (on 1 Tim 3:8-16), 1

Paul[14] has discussed bishops, listed their attributes, and said which qualities they should possess and which they should shun. He omits the order of presbyters, and passes to the deacons. Why? Because there was not much difference between presbyters and bishops. Presbyters, too, have undertaken the office of teaching and of leadership in the church. What he said about bishops is appropriate for them also. Bishops are superior only in the power of ordination; only by this do they seem to excel the presbyters.

"Likewise the deacons" [1 Tim 3:8]. That is, he says, they must have the same qualities as bishops. What are they? To be blameless, sober, hospitable, patient, peaceable, not greedy. He wants them to be the same because he says "likewise"; this is clear from his specific examples, when he says, "serious, not double-tongued" [ibid.], that is, not deceitful or treacherous. Nothing usually so debases men as treachery; nothing is so unseemly in the church as deceit. He continues: "Not addicted to much wine, not greedy for gain, holding the mystery of the faith with a clear conscience" [1 Tim 3:8-9]. See, he has shown what it means to be blameless. And notice how he puts "and not a neophyte" here, too. In saying, "Let these also be tested first" [1 Tim 3:10], as he had said concerning the bishop, he has added the conjunction "also" with nothing standing in between. This is also why he says there, "not a neophyte." How could it not be absurd, if a newly purchased slave is not entrusted with anything within the house until he gives abundant witness through a thorough testing of his judgment, but one coming into God's Church from outside were immediately given the highest rank?

[14]Text: PG 62.553-554.

"Likewise the women":—he means deaconesses—
"serious, not double-tongued, sober, faithful in everything"
[1 Tim 3:11]. Some say that he says this simply about
women, but that is not the case. For why would he wish to
add something about women to what he has already said?
He is speaking about those women who have the dignity of
the diaconate.

"Let the deacons be the husbands of one wife" [1 Tim
3:12]. These words are also appropriately said of women
deacons. This office is quite necessary and useful and fitting
in the church. "Let the deacons be the husbands of one
wife," he says. Do you see how he demands the same virtue
from deacons also? Even if they are not of the same dignity
as the bishop, they must also be equally blameless and holy.

"Let them manage their children and their households
well. Those who have served well as deacons gain a good
standing for themselves, and great confidence in the faith in
Christ Jesus" [1 Tim 3:12-13]. He puts down the right
upbringing of children everywhere, lest the others are scandalized for this reason. "Those who have served well as
deacons," he says, "gain a good standing for themselves"—
that is, advancement, and "great confidence in the faith of
Jesus Christ," as if he were saying, those who have shown
themselves attentive will quickly rise to higher ranks.

11. Theodore of Mopsuestia
Catechetical Homily 15, 18-27

[Tr. by A. Mingana]

Theodore, born ca. 352 in Antioch, was a long-time
friend of John Chrysostom. After some years in a monastery, he was ordained a presbyter, and, in 392, bishop of
Mopsuestia in Cilicia. He died in that office in 428. He
wrote commentaries on almost all the books of the Bible,
and many dogmatic treatises. Because he was later asso-
ciated with Nestorianism, however, most of his writings
perished in Greek; much of what remains is preserved in

Syriac. The excerpt that follows is from a work discovered by A. Mingana in the early twentieth century. In these homilies for catechumens and the newly baptized, Theodore explained the creed, the liturgy of baptism, and the Eucharist. They were probably composed between 388 and 392, when he was a presbyter in Antioch. The passage which follows vividly describes the ministry of priests and deacons at the Eucharist in a typically Antiochene fashion.

[18.][15] As the real new birth is the one which we expect through the resurrection, and we nevertheless perform this new birth symbolically and sacramentally through baptism, so also the real food of immortality is that which we hope to receive truly in heaven by the grace of the Holy Spirit, but now we symbolically eat the immortal food which is given to us by the grace of the Holy Spirit, whether in symbols or through symbols. 19. It follows that a role of a high priest must needs be filled, and it is found in those who are appointed for the service of these symbols. Those who have been chosen as the priests of the New Testament are believed to perform sacramentally, by the descent of the Holy Spirit, and for the confirmation and admonition of the children of the sacrament, these things which we believe that Christ our Lord performed and will perform in reality.

This is the reason why they do not immolate at all times new sacrifices like the priests of the law. These were ordered to offer to God numerous and different sacrifices of oxen, goats and sheep, and offered new sacrifices at all times. When first sacrificial beasts had been slaughtered, had died and suffered complete dissolution, others were always immolated in the place of those which had been slaughtered a long time previously. As to the priests of the New Testament they immolate the same sacrifice always and everywhere, because one is the sacrifice which has been immolated for us, that of Christ our Lord who suffered

---

[15]Trans.: Commentary of Theodore of Mopsuestia and the Lord's Prayer and on the Sacraments of Baptism and the Eucharist, by A. Mingana (Cambridge, 1933).

death for us and who, by his offering this sacrifice, obtained perfection for us, as the blessed Paul said: "By one offering he perfected for ever them that are sanctified" [Heb 10:14]. **20.** All of us, everywhere, at all times, and always, observe the commemoration of that sacrifice, "for as often as we eat this bread and drink this cup we do show the Lord's death till he come" [1 Cor 11:26]. As often, therefore, as the service of this awe-inspiring sacrifice is performed, which is clearly the likeness of heavenly things and of which, after it has been perfected, we become worthy to partake through food and drink, as a true participation in our future benefits—we must picture in our mind that we are dimly in heaven, and, through faith, draw in our imagination the image of heavenly things, while thinking that Christ who is in heaven and who died for us, rose and ascended into heaven and is now being immolated. In contemplating with our eyes, through faith, the facts that are now being re-enacted: that he is again dying, rising and ascending into heaven, we shall be led to the vision of the things that had taken place beforehand on our behalf.

21. Because Christ our Lord offered himself in sacrifice for us and thus became our high priest in reality, we must think that the priest who draws nigh unto the altar is representing his image, not that he offers himself in sacrifice, any more than he is truly a high priest, but because he performs the figure of the service of the ineffable sacrifice of Christ, and through this figure he dimly represents the image of the unspeakable heavenly things and of the supernatural and incorporeal hosts. Indeed, all the invisible hosts did service to that economy which transcends our words and which Christ our Lord accomplished for us. "They are all ministering spirits sent forth to minister for them who shall be heirs of salvation" [Heb 1:14] as the blessed Paul said. Matthew, the evangelist, showed also this when he said: "And the angels came and ministered unto him" [Matt 4:11]. This is also attested by our Lord who said: "Hereafter you shall see heaven open and the angels of God ascending and descending to the Son of man" [John 1:51]. Incidents in the gospel show also events that happened through them, whether it be through those who at the birth of our Lord sang: "Glory to God in the highest, peace on earth and good hope to men" [Luke 2:14], or through those who at his resurrection revealed to women what had occurred, or through those who at his ascension explained to the apostles that which they did not know. It is necessary, therefore, that here also, when this awe-inspiring service is performed, we should think that the deacons represent an image of the service of these invisible spirits, and that they have been appointed to minister unto this awe-inspiring service by the grace of the Holy Spirit which they received.

22. This is the reason why all of us are called the ministers of Christ, as the blessed Paul said: "Inasmuch as I am the apostle of the Gentiles I magnify my ministry"[Rom 11:13]. This name, however, is especially applied to those who perform this ministry, and are called by all "deacons," as they are alone appointed to perform this ministry, and represent a likeness of the service of the spiritual messengers and ministers. **23.** They have also an apparel which is consonant with their office, since their outer garment is taller than they are, as wearing such an apparel in such a way is suitable to those who serve. They place on their left shoulders a stole, which floats equally on either side, forwards and backwards. This is a sign that they are not performing a ministry of servitude but of freedom, as they are ministering unto things that lead to freedom all those who are worthy of the great house of God, that is to say, the Church. They do not place the stole on their neck in a way that it floats on either side but not in front, because there is no one serving in a house who wears such an apparel; it is only those who are masters of themselves and remote from servitude of any kind who wear it in this way, but deacons place it on their shoulders because they are appointed for service. The stole is their only sign of that freedom to which all of us, who believed in Christ, have been called; and we hasten to go to, and be in, "the house of God, which is the Church of the living God, the pillar and ground of the truth" [1 Tim 3:15], as the blessed Paul says; and they are clearly appointed for the service of all things performed in it.

24. Because the things performed for us by Christ our Lord are awe-inspiring, and because we expect their complete fulfilment in the next world, we receive them now only by faith, and we proceed gradually in this world in a way that we are in nothing absent from our faith in them. This being the case, we are necessarily confirmed in the faith of the things revealed to us through this ministry of the sacrament, as we are led through it to the future reality, because it contains an image of the ineffable economy of Christ our Lord, in which we receive the vision and the shadow of the happenings that took place. This is the reason why through the priest we picture Christ our Lord in our mind, as through him we see the one who saved us and delivered us by the sacrifice of himself; and through the deacons who serve the things that take place, we picture in our mind the invisible hosts who served with that ineffable service. It is the deacons who bring out this oblation—or the symbols of this oblation—which they arrange and place on the awe-inspiring altar, and oblation which in its vision, as represented in the imagination, is an awe-inspiring event to the onlookers.

25. We must also think of Christ being at one time led and brought to his passion, and at another time stretched on the altar to be sacrificed for us. And when the offering which is about to be placed on the altar is brought out in the sacred vessels of the paten and the chalice, we must think that Christ our Lord is being led and brought to his passion, not, however, by the Jews—as it is incongruous and impermissible that an iniquitous image be found in the symbols of our deliverance and our salvation—but by the invisible hosts of ministry, who are sent to us and who were also present when the passion of our salvation was being accomplished, and were doing their service. Indeed, they performed their service to all the economy of Christ our Lord without any exception, and were present with their service at the time of the passion, endeavoring to perform it according to the will of God. When our Lord was in deep thought and fear at the approach of his passion, the blessed Luke said that "an angel appeared unto him strengthening and encouraging him" [Luke 22:43], and like those persons who are wont to stir up the courage of the athletes with their voices, he anointed him to bear tribulations, and by encouraging words persuaded him to endure pains with patience, and showed him that his passion was small in comparison with the benefit that will accrue from it, as he would be invested with great glory after his passion and his death, from which he would be the cause of numerous benefits not only to men but to all the creation.

We must think, therefore, that the deacons who now carry the Eucharistic bread and bring it out for the sacrifice represent the image of the invisible hosts of ministry, with this difference, that, through their ministry and in these remembrances, they do not send Christ our Lord to his salvation-giving passion. 26. When they bring out the Eucharistic bread they place it on the holy altar, for the complete representation of the passion, so that we may think of him on the altar, as if he were placed in the sepulcher, after having received his passion. This is the reason why those deacons who spread linens on the altar represent the figure of the linen clothes of the burial of our Lord. Sometime after these have been spread, they stand up on both sides, and agitate all the air above the holy body with fans, thus keeping it from any defiling object. They make manifest by this ritual the greatness of the body which is lying there, as it is the habit, when the dead body of the high personages of this world is carried on a bier, that some men should fan the air above it. It is, therefore, with justice that the same thing is done here with the body which lies on the altar, and which is holy, awe-inspiring and remote from all corruption; a body which will very shortly rise to an immortal nature.

It is on all sides of this body that persons, who are especially appointed to serve, stand up and fan. They offer to it an honor that is suitable, and by this ritual they make manifest to those present the greatness of the sacred body that is lying there. 27. It is indeed clear to us from the divine book that angels sat upon the stone near the sepulcher and announced his resurrection to the women, and remained there all the time of his death, in honor of the one who was laid there, till they witnessed the resurrection, which was proclaimed by them to be good to all mankind, and to imply a renewal of all the creation, as the blessed Paul said: "Any man who is in Christ is a new creature. Old things are passed away and all things are become new" [2 Cor 5:17].

Was it not right, therefore, that here also the deacons should represent as in an image the ministry of the angels? It is in remembrance of those who constantly came to the passion and death of our Lord, that they also stand in a circle and agitate the air with fans, and offer honor and adoration to the sacred and awe-inspiring body which is lying there. In this they make manifest to all those present the greatness of the object that is lying there, and induce all the onlookers to think of it as awe-inspiring and truly sacred, and to realize that it is for this reason that they keep it from all defiling things, and do not even allow the dirty tricklings of birds to fall upon it and come near it. This they do now according to their habit in order to show that because the body which is lying there is high, awe-inspiring, holy, and truly Lord through its union with the divine nature, it is with great fear that it must be handled, seen and kept.

12. Pseudo-Eusebius of Alexandria
Sermon 5

"Eusebius of Alexandria" is the pseudonym assigned to the author of a collection of sermons, written in Greek, which probably date from the late fifth or early sixth century. No internal evidence connects them with the city of Alexandria. The fifth sermon, translated here, presupposes that a presbyter is the pastor of a parish; he is assisted by a deacon, and the deacon replaces him in his absence. The deacon may not celebrate the Eucharist, but does distribute the consecrated elements left by the presbyter. As in other documents, here too the role of the presbyter as guide and guardian of the people's morals is stressed.

1.[16] Our Savior, lover of men, takes pity on our race and does not send anyone away with no share in his grace, for grace is given not only to the just but also to sinners. Since he is not envious and no respecter of persons, makes the sun rise on the wicked and on the good, sends rain upon the just and the unjust, and wills that all men should be saved, he does not overlook the sinner, but gives even him a little grace so that he will revere the giver and thank him, and turn around and be converted. But if he should accept the grace and still remain in his sins, then even the grace which he has left will be taken from him and he will be condemned to the Gehenna of fire, because he did not revere either the honor he received or the one who honored him. And the word of Scripture is fulfilled against him: "If a man is honored and does not acknowledge it, he is similar to the unthinking beasts and has become like them" [Ps 49:12].

2. I know sinful priests who have laid hands on sick people and have cured them. But cures take place for two reasons, and involve not only the giver, but also the receiver. For if it is not in faith that a man receives something, he will not accept it from an unjust man; but the believer receives the grace of healing immediately, even from a sinner. The unbeliever receives the grace neither from a just man nor from a sinner, for to each is given according to his faith. The Lord said to those who came to him, "Let it be done to you according to your faith" [Matt 9:29]. Believe in the Lord's name as you approach, and do not be condemned in any way, and you will receive the grace of healing, for it is God who works. There are many sinful priests who offer the gifts and God is not turned away. By the Holy Spirit he sanctifies the gifts which were set forth; and the bread becomes the body, and the cup becomes the blood of our Lord Jesus Christ. And there are some who assume that they are doing

[16]Text: PG 86.341-349.

something praiseworthy, and have no communion with the presbyters because they know of some sin committed by the presbyter. And they do not know that they sin all the more because they wish to do good.

3. For who are you, who judge the presbyter? Who are you who judge your ruler? And again: "Who are you who judge another man's slave? By his own lord he has stood, and he falls, but he will rather be made to stand, for God is able to make him stand" [Rom 14:4]. You are taught and guided by Paul; you do not have the power to judge or condemn him. Have you not heard the Apostle, who says, "You must not speak evil of the ruler of the people" [Acts 23:5]? And again he said, "Do not judge before the time, until the Lord comes; he will make known the counsels of the heart, and then approval will come from God" [1 Cor 4:5]. The presbyter has the power to judge you; the one who judges him is the Lord. And again the Lord says: "Do not judge, so that you will not be judged" [Matt 7:1]. Pay due honor and reverence, and fulfill the prescriptions of the law. Offer the first fruits of your firstlings. Do not withhold what is owed to the church; give; do not investigate how your gift is spent. If you attempt to judge the presbyter, first search out the storeroom of your heart, test yourself to see whether you have anything bad on your conscience, or whether your judgment condemns you. And I do not tell you to search through the evil deeds of all your years, but of one day only. Examine carefully how the day went: whether your eye was scandalized in any way; whether you disregarded a poor man; whether you derided your neighbor, or mocked him. See whether any of these faults harmed your soul. If you are free of all of them, and are clean, it is still not good to make an accusation against the presbyter or against your neighbor. "But," someone says, "he has fornicated." But you have stolen from your neighbor and taken from the poor man. Let each one consider the evil in his own works and not look around at his neighbor who searches thus. If someone accidentally hears what is said and should engage his own tongue in accusing a presbyter or anyone else, let him expect the same recompense; for what one does to his neighbor, that he should expect to undergo. And if you do such things, do you search out your neighbor's sins? He says to you rightly, "Hypocrite, first cast the beam out of your eyes, and then you will look at the speck in your brother's eye" [Matt 7:5]. Meditate on your own sins; do not judge what you are not appointed to judge.

4. Otherwise the presbyter ought to be disposed thus toward the people: before all else he should pray with his whole soul for the people; he should be in charge of their affairs until his death; and he should lay down his life for his flock. The Lord meant this when he said, "The good shepherd lays down his life for his sheep" [John 10:11]. The presbyter should help the man in need, console the grieving, and particularly not remember old injuries, for the presbyter who carries a grudge sins every day. The prayer of one who carries a grudge is never carried pure to God, for the evil fills his whole heart. If you do not put an end to the evil do not approach the altar. Remember what the Lord commanded you when he said, "If you bring your gift to the altar and there remember your brother, withdraw, be reconciled with your brother, and so come and offer your gift" [Matt 5:23-24]. Do not disregard the voice of the Master who speaks to you, lest you be condemned. Care for your servants; do not humiliate one and exalt the other, or hold one in esteem and disregard the other. Do not honor the rich man with the first places at table and neglect the poor man who cannot offer you gifts; but preserve equality in all things. Do not accept accusations quickly, and never judge on what you have heard; many condemn their neighbor out of jealousy and rivalry. If, after taking every caution, you find that someone is a sinner, do not accuse him immediately before all, lest you give him an occasion for excessive shame. To accuse a man before all has two evils. Some who are reproached cannot bear the shame or put up with grief and disgrace; they yield to the other evil, especially when they are reproached at the wrong time, and turn to death by hanging. This is the way the devil acts: he suggests that someone should do evil, and after the one sin is committed he urges him to commit others. And after the man commits them, the devil laughs in scorn, and prepares trials and accusers; he prepares to charge others with that mistake, and he becomes both defender and accuser. He both conquers the man who was accused while he is still inclined to madness, and also instigates the great shame and contrives the hanging.

5. Because of these snares of the Evil One, you who are entrusted with Christ's spiritual flock must be long-suffering, and should seek after great stability. And when you discover someone who has sinned, do not eject him from the church immediately, lest Satan lay hold of the man and make him his own. Whenever the man is separated from the priest, Satan immediately embraces him, and once he has received him he cannot be parted from him. The priest should not exclude anyone frequently, nor curse anyone, nor reject a sinner forthwith. You the shepherd know this; you should not reject the sheep, nor separate it from the flock; but whenever you find a sinner, call him apart. Reprove some things, encourage him in others, and remind him a second and third time to abstain from evil. If he hears you and abstains from sin, you have won his soul, just as the Scripture says: "The one who converts the sinner from his erring way will cover a multitude of sins" [Jas 5:20]. Concede him his first sins. The one who forgives will be forgiven. And again the Lord, lover of men, said that if your brother sins against you seventy-seven times, forgive him and never reproach him with his secret sins, nor provoke him when he repents. If he disobeys you after three warnings and remains in the same sins, then finally accuse him before all, so that all might reprove him at your command. And if he disobeys all and does not set his life right, cut him off from yourself and do not take a meal with such a man until he has corrected himself through a change of heart, and then finally he will be received back. The priest must know all of these things; and also how he must conduct himself in regard to the people; and then he will not be condemned for eternity.

6. Finally I will set out the teaching concerning deacons. Now the deacon must do everything according to the presbyter's judgment, in regard both to canonical law and to

ecclesiastical customs. Let him have no authority over the people, but do everything at the bidding of the presbyter. When the presbyter is present he has no power to excommunicate anyone or to do anything else. If the priest is not present he has power over everything just as a priest does, apart from the holy gifts and mysteries. If the priest is ever going to be away from home he should call in a presbyter from another village to offer the prayers for the people. But if there is no presbyter, a priest should consecrate bread and instruct the deacon to distribute it to the people. If a child is found unbaptized, and the child is about to die, the deacon has the authority to baptize it. But if a child comes to be baptized, and dies without baptism through the carelessness of the presbyter, woe to that presbyter! If it dies unbaptized through the neglect of the parents, the priest escapes blameless, but woe to the parents of the child! The parents clearly must not keep a child unbaptized for a very long time, for a sheep without the seal belongs to the wolf. Everyone who guards the flock has fulfilled the command of Christ. [Here the blessed one ended his discourse.] Amen.

3. THE CHURCH IN THE WESTERN EMPIRE

13. Tertullian

Tertullian was born in Carthage ca. 160. He was well educated, and equally fluent in Latin and Greek. He may have been converted to Christianity in Rome; in any case, he left Rome in 195 already a Christian, and returned to his native Carthage, where he died sometime after 220. Ca. 207 he joined the strict Montanist sect, and his later writings show this influence. Tertullian was the first Christian to write extensively in Latin and he, in many ways, formed the Latin vocabulary of Christianity. He is almost always polemical, and often sarcastic. The short excerpts that follow illustrate different attitudes on Tertullian's part. The first, from his work *On the Prescription of Heretics*, written ca. 200, defends the need for order in the church by satirizing the disorder among sectarians. The excerpts from *On Baptism* treat the minister of this sacrament. The work *On Purity* is from his Montanist period; here Tertullian argues vigorously against the ecclesiastical hierarchy established by succession, and in favor of a "charismatic" hierarchy.

ON THE PRESCRIPTION OF HERETICS, 41

[Tr. by S. L. Greenslade]

I[1] must not leave out a description of the heretics' way of life—futile, earthly, all too human, lacking in gravity, in authority, in discipline, as suits their faith. To begin with, one cannot tell who is a catechumen and who is baptized. They come in together, listen together, pray together. Even if any of the heathen arrive, they are quite willing to cast that which is holy to the dogs and their pearls (false ones!) before swine. The destruction of discipline is to them simplicity, and our attention to it they call affectation. They are in communion with everyone everywhere. Differences of theology are of no concern to them as long as they are all agreed in attacking the truth. They are all puffed up, they all promise knowledge. Their catechumens are perfect before they are fully instructed. As for the women of the heretics, how forward they are! They have the impudence to teach, to argue, to perform exorcisms, to promise cures, perhaps even to baptize. Their ordinations are hasty, irresponsible and unstable. Sometimes they appoint novices, sometimes men tied to secular office, sometimes renegades from us, hoping to bind them by ambition as they cannot bind them by the truth. Nowhere can you get quicker promotion than in the camp of the rebels, where your mere presence is a merit. So one man is bishop today, another tomorrow. The deacon of today is tomorrow's reader, the priest of today is tomorrow a layman. For they impose priestly functions even upon laymen.

ON BAPTISM 7; 17

[Tr. by Ernest Evans]

7.[2] After that we come up from the washing and are anointed with the blessed unction, following that ancient

[1]Text: SC 46.146-148, ed. by R. F. Refoulé (1957). Trans.; *Early Latin Theology*, by S. L. Greenslade, (Philadelphia, 1956), 61-62.

[2]Text: SC 35.76,89-91, ed. by R. F. Refoulé (1952). Trans.: *Tertullian's Homily on Baptism*, by Ernest Evans, (London' 1964), 17, 35-37.

practice by which, ever since Aaron was anointed by Moses, there was a custom of anointing them for priesthood with oil out of a horn. That is why the high priest is called a christ, from "chrism" which is the Greek for "anointing": and from this also our Lord obtained his title, though it had become a spiritual anointing, in that he was anointed with the Spirit by God the Father: and so it says in the Acts, "For a truth they are gathered together in this city against your holy Son whom you have anointed" [Acts 4:27]. So also in our case, the unction flows upon the flesh, but turns to spiritual profit, just as in the baptism itself there is an act that touches the flesh, that we are immersed in water, but a spiritual effect, that we are set free from sins.

17. To round off our slight treatment of this subject it remains for me to advise you of the rules to be observed in giving and receiving baptism. The supreme right of giving it belongs to the high priest, which is the bishop: after him, to the presbyters and deacons, yet not without commission from the bishop, on account of the Church's dignity: for when this is safe, peace is safe. Except for that, even laymen have the right: for that which is received on equal terms can be given on equal terms: unless perhaps you are prepared to allege that our Lord's disciples were already bishops or presbyters or deacons: that is, as the word ought not to be hidden by any man, so likewise baptism, which is no less declared to be "of God," can be administered by all. Yet how much rather are the rules of humility and restraint incumbent upon laymen, seeing they apply to greater persons, who must not arrogate to themselves the function of the bishop. Opposition to the episcopate is the mother of schisms. The holy apostle has said that all things are lawful but all things are not expedient: which means it is enough that you should use this right in emergencies, if ever conditions of place or time or person demand it. The boldness of a rescuer is acceptable when he is constrained to it by the necessities of the man in peril, since he will be guilty of a man's destruction if he forbears to give the help he is free and able to give. But the impudence of that woman who assumed the right to teach is evidently not going to arrogate to her the right to baptize as well—unless perhaps some new serpent appears, like that original one, so that as that woman abolished baptism, some other should of her own authority confer it. But if certain Acts of Paul,[3] which are falsely so named, claim the example of Thecla for allowing women to teach and to baptize, let men know that in Asia the presbyter who compiled that document, thinking to add of his own to Paul's reputation, was found out, and though he professed he had done it for love of Paul, was deposed from his position. How could we believe that Paul should give a female power to teach and to baptize, when he did not allow a woman even to learn by her own right? "Let them keep silence," he says, "and ask their husbands at home" [1 Cor 14:35].

ON PURITY, 21

[Tr. by William P. LeSaint]

Since[4] the apostles understood this better than others, naturally they were more solicitous about it than others. And now, at length, I come to that point in my argument where I make a distinction between the *doctrine* of the apostles and their *power*. Doctrine gives direction to a man; power marks him out with a special character. The power of the Spirit is a thing apart, for the Spirit is God. What, then, did He teach? "There must be no fellowship with works of darkness" [Eph 5:11]. Observe His commandment! And who had power to forgive sins? This no one can do but He Himself: "For who forgives sins but God alone?" [Mark 2:7]. This means, of course, mortal sins committed against Him and against His temple. For as far as you yourself are

---

[3]An English translation of the extant parts of this second-century work is found in E. Hennecke, *New Testament Apocryphya*, II (London, 1965). Tertullian wrote *On Baptism* to refute a woman who taught that baptism was unnecessary.

[4]Text: CCL 2.1326-28, ed. by E. Dekkers (1954). Trans.: *Treatises on Penance*, by W. P. LeSaint (ACW 28; Westminster, 1959), 118-122.

concerned, you are commanded in the person of Peter to forgive offenses committed against yourself even seventy times seven times.

Therefore if it were proved that the blessed apostles themselves showed indulgence to any sin of such a character that it could be pardoned by God alone and not by man, they would have done this because power was given them and not because doctrine allowed it. Moreover, the apostles raised the dead to life, something which God alone can do. They healed the sick, something which no one but Christ can do. They even inflicted punishments, something which Christ did not wish to do, for it was not fitting that He should strike who came to suffer. Ananias was smitten and Elymas also, Ananias with death and Elymas with blindness; this itself proves that Christ, too, had the power to do these things.

So it was with the prophets also. They pardoned murder—and adultery which was joined with it—to those who were penitent; this was justified by the fact that they also gave proof of their severity. Now then, apostolic man, show me samples of your prophetic works so that I may recognize your divine authorization; after this, claim for yourself the power to forgive such sins. If, however, you have been entrusted with no office beyond that of teaching moral doctrine, and if your presidential authority is that of a servant and not a master, then who do you think you are, or how exalted, that you grant pardon for sin? You show yourself neither prophet nor apostle; therefore you lack the power in virtue of which pardon is granted.

"But the Church," you say, "has power to forgive sins." I know this better than you do and I regulate it better, because I have the Paraclete Himself saying in the person of the new prophets:[5] "The Church can forgive sin, but I will not do it lest others also sin." But what if a false prophetic spirit said this? This can not be the case, since the Destroyer would

---

[5]The "new prophets" are the enthusiastic revivalists, Montanus and his companions Maximilla and Prisca. There is an English translation of their extant oracles in Robert M. Grant, *Second-Century Christianity: A Collection of Fragments* (London, 1946).

rather have commended himself by his clemency and he would have set others in the way of sin. Or if, here too, he tried to ape the Spirit of truth, then the Spirit of truth can, indeed, grant pardon to fornication but will not do it when it brings harm to many.

And now I put a question to you about this opinion of yours: Where do you get this right which you claim for your Church? If it is because the Lord said to Peter: "Upon this rock I will build by Church; I have given you the keys of the kingdom of heaven"; or: "Whatsoever you shall bind or lose on earth, will be bound or loosed in heaven" [Matt 16:18-19], then you presume that the power of binding and loosing has devolved upon you also, that is, upon every church which is akin to Peter. Who are you to pervert and to change completely the manifest will of Christ, who grants this to Peter personally? "Upon you," he says, "I will build my Church"; and, "I will give the keys to you," not to the Church; and, "Whatsoever you shall loose or bind," not what they shall loose or bind.

This is also clear from the sequel. In him was the Church built, that is, through him. He himself first used the key—and see what it was: "Men of Israel, give ear to what I say. Jesus of Nazareth, a man destined for you by God" etc. [Acts 2:22]. He himself, thereafter, was the first to open the gate of the kingdom of heaven in the Baptism of Christ, wherein sins are "loosed" which were formerly "bound" and those are "bound" which were not loosed in the way of true salvation. Besides this, he "bound" Ananias in the bonds of death, and he also "loosed" the lame man from his crippling disease. Moreover, in that well-known dispute about the observance of the Law, Peter was the first of all to be moved by the Spirit, and after some introductory remarks on the vocation of the Gentiles, he said: "And now why do you tempt the Lord in this matter of putting a yoke on the brethren which neither we nor our fathers were able to bear? But we believe that it is through the grace of Jesus that we will be saved, just as they" [Acts 15:10-11]. This statement both loosed the precepts of the Law which were abrogated and, at the same time, it bound those which remained in force. We conclude, then, that the power of loosing and binding which was committed to Peter has nothing to do with forgiving the capital sins of the faithful.

Since Christ told him to forgive even seventy times seven times a brother who offended him, certainly he would not afterwards have commanded him to bind anything, that is, to retain it, except, perhaps, such sins as a man might commit against the Lord and not against a brother. For the fact that it is sins against man which are pardoned, settles it antecedently that those committed against God must not be pardoned.

What, then, does this have to do with the Church, and I mean yours, you Sensualist? For this power is Peter's personally and, after that, it belongs to those who have the Spirit—to an apostle or a prophet. For the Church is itself, properly and principally, the Spirit Himself, in whom there is a trinity of one divinity, Father, Son and Holy Spirit. He unites in one congregation that Church which the Lord said consists of three persons. And so, from this time on, any number of persons at all, joined in this faith, is recognized as the Church by Him who founded and consecrated it. Therefore it is true that the Church will pardon sins, but this is the Church of the Spirit, through a man who has the Spirit; it is not the Church which consists of a number of bishops. For it is the Lord and not the servant who has this sovereign right. It belongs to God Himself, not to a priest.

14. Cyprian of Carthage

Cyprian was born in Carthage ca. 200 and converted to Christianity in 246. In 248 or 249 he was elected bishop of his city, the most important in north Africa. In 250 the persecution of Decius began, and Cyprian temporarily withdrew from the city, a decision which later caused him some embarrassment. In the ten years in which he was bishop, he wrote numerous shorter works and letters, many of them dealing with the church and its organization. He died a martyr in the persecution of Valerian

(258). Of the letters presented here, letter 3 advises a bishop on how to deal with a rebellious deacon. In letter 38, written during his absence from Carthage in 250, Cyprian explains to his church why he ordained someone a lector without consulting them. In the excerpt from letter 55, he defends the ordination of Cornelius of Rome. The passage from letter 67 deals with the ordination of men who had fallen away during the persecutions.

Cyprian stresses that the unity of the Church is visible in the college of legitimately ordained bishops. On the one hand, he simply identifies the apostles as bishops, and emphasizes the immediate institution of the episcopacy by Christ. He applies the prescriptions of the Old Testament directly to the Christian episcopacy, and makes freedom from taint of apostasy a condition for legitimacy in the episcopal office. On the other hand, he also insists on the role of the people in the choice of bishops and other clergy, and even writes cautiously to his congregation to explain why he ordained a lector without consulting them.

LETTER 3

Cyprian greets his brother Rogatianus.

1.[6] I and the colleagues who were present were deeply and painfully shaken, dearest brother, when we read your letter. You complained about your deacon, that he was unmindful of your priestly rank and of his own office and ministry and afflicted you with his insults and affronts. You acted honorably in respect to us and with your usual humility when you preferred to register a complaint about him with us, although by the right to jurisdiction of the episcopal office and the authority of your rank you had the power which enabled you to discipline him immediately. You could be sure that all of us, your colleagues, would accept whatever you did by your priestly authority in the case of

[6]Text: CSEL 3.2,469–472, ed. by W. Hartel (1871).

your insolent deacon. We have divine commandments about men of this sort, for the Lord God says in Deuteronomy: "And whichever man should act in pride and not obey a priest or a judge, whoever he is in those days, that man will die, and the whole people will fear when they hear about it, and they will not act irreverently even now" [Deut 17:12-13].

So that we might know that this command of God, that his priests should be revered and vindicated, was proclaimed with true and highest authority, we have this example: when Korah, Dathan and Abiram, three ministers of Aaron the priest, dared to act haughtily against him and lift up their necks and to make themselves equal to the priest placed over them, they were absorbed and swallowed up by a gaping hole in the earth and immediately suffered the punishment for their sacrilegious pride. And besides these three, two hundred and fifty others who were their companions in insolence were consumed by a fire that burst forth from the Lord in order to prove that priests of God are avenged by him who makes them priests. And in the book of Kingdoms, when the priest Samuel was disdained by the Jewish people because of his old age—just as you were disdained—the Lord was angry and cried out and said, "They did not spurn you, but they spurn me" [1 Sam 8:7]. And to avenge this he raised up Saul as king, to strike them with mortal wounds and to trample on that haughty people and to afflict them for all their insults and the suffering they caused. Thus the priest who was insulted by the haughty nation was vindicated by divine vengeance.

2. Solomon too, inspired by the Holy Spirit, bears witness and teaches what the priestly authority and power are when he says, "Fear God with your whole soul, and treat his priests as holy" [Sir 7, 29]. And, "Reverence God with your whole heart, and honor his priests" [Sir 7, 31]. As we read in the Acts of the Apostles, the blessed Apostle was mindful of these commandments; when he was told "Do you attack the priest of God thus with abuse?" he answered and said, "I did not know, brethren, that he is the high priest. For it is written, 'You shall not abuse the prince of your people' " [Acts 23:4-5]. Even our Lord Jesus Christ, King and Judge and our God, held the high priests and the priests in honor up until the day of His passion, although they showed Him neither fear, as God, nor recognition, as the Christ. For when He had cleansed the leper He said to him, "Go and show yourself to the priest and offer a gift" [Matt 8:4]. He still called the one whom he knew to be impious a priest, with that humility by which He also taught us to be humble. Likewise when He suffered His passion, He received a slap and someone said to Him, "Do you answer the high priest thus?" He said nothing insolent against the person of the high priest, but rather defended His innocence and said, "If I have spoken ill, charge me with the evil; but if I have spoken well, why do you strike me?" [John 18:23]. He did all of this humbly and patiently to give us a model of humility and patience. He taught that true priests should be revered legitimately and fully, while doing just this in regard to false priests.

3. But deacons should remember that the Lord chose the apostles—that is, the bishops and leaders, whereas the apostles established the deacons for themselves after the Lord's ascension into heaven, as servants of their episcopal office and of the church. But if we can rebel against God, who makes bishops, then deacons can rebel against us, by whom they are made. And so the deacon whom you write about should do penance for his insolence, to acknowledge the honor of the priest and to make reparation in full humility to the bishop placed over him. For these are the beginnings of heretics, and the birth and endeavor of schismatics who think evil: how they may please themselves, how they might defy their superior in their swollen pride. Thus they draw away from the church, thus they build a profane altar outside, thus they rebel against Christ's peace and the decree and unity of God. But if he afflicts and provokes you with his abuse, you will use the power of your office against him and either depose him or excommunicate him. For if the apostle Paul, writing to Timothy, said, "Let no one despise your youth" [1 Tim 4:12], how much more should your colleagues say to you, "Let no one despise your old age." And since you wrote that someone else has involved himself

with that same deacon of yours and shares in his pride and insolence, you will be able either to restrain or to excommunicate this man too, along with any others who are thus and act against God's priest. The alternative, which we urge and admonish them to, is that they realize that they have sinned, make satisfaction, and allow us to stand by our purpose. For we hope and desire to conquer the insults and injuries of individuals with kindness and patience, rather than to punish them with priestly authority. Dearest brother, I hope you are always well.

LETTER 38

Cyprian greets the presbyters, deacons, and the whole people, his brethren.

1. [7] In the ordinations of clerics, dear brethren, we usually consult you beforehand and weigh the morals and merits of individuals in common council. But we need not wait for human testimony when divine approbation is already present. Our brother Aurelius, a distinguished young man, has already been tested by the Lord and is dear to God. In years he is still young, but in his praiseworthy virtue and faith he is already advanced. He is younger in his natural years, but older in honor. He has struggled in a double contest. He twice confessed the faith and was twice glorified by the victory of his confession, both when he triumphed by being exiled in the first contest and when he once more fought to a victory in a fiercer struggle and conquered in the battle of suffering. As often as the adversary wished to provoke the servants of God, so often this well-prepared and brave soldier both fought and won. It was a small thing, when he was made an exile, to do battle first before the eyes of a few. He deserved to fight with more illustrious virtue in the forum and so afterwards to defeat magistrates and a proconsul, and after exile to withstand torture.

[7]Text: CSEL, 3,2,579-581.

I do not know what I should praise in him more, the glory of his wounds or the modesty of his manners. Should I praise him because he is distinguished by honorable virtue, or because he is praiseworthy on account of his admirable modesty? He is thus both so exalted by his dignity and so gentle in his humility that it is clear that he has been divinely spared to be an example to others for ecclesiastical discipline, to show how servants of God can triumph in confession by their virtues and afterwards surpass their confession by their morals.

2. Such a man deserved the higher ranks of clerical ordination and greater advancement; he should be judged not by his age but by his merits. But for the time being it seemed right that he should begin with the office of lector. There is nothing more fitting than that a voice which confessed God in glorious proclamation should resound in proclaiming the divine readings; that after his sublime words which declared the martyrdom of Christ, he should read the gospel of Christ which is the wellspring of martyrs. It is fitting that after the scaffold he should approach the lectern. At the scaffold he stood before a crowd of unbelievers; at the lectern he is seen by the brethren. At the scaffold he was heard with amazement by the people standing about; at the lectern he is heard with joy by the brethren.

Know, therefore, dear brothers, that this man was ordained by me and by those colleagues who were present. I know that you will embrace him joyfully and hope that as many such men as possible will be ordained in our church. And since happiness is always in a hurry, and joy can bear no delays, he reads for us on Sunday—that is, he initiates peace while he proclaims the reading. Devote yourselves to prayer, and help our prayers with your own, praying that the Lord's mercy which protects us might bring back the priest to his people unharmed and the martyr-lector with that priest. Dear brethren, I hope you are always well.

LETTER 55, 8-10

Cyprian greets his brother Antonianus.

8.[8] Now, dearest brother, I come to write of the person of our colleague Cornelius,[9] in order that, like us, you might know him more accurately—not from the lies of malicious detractors, but from the judgment of God, who made him a bishop, and the testimony of his fellow bishops, whose total number throughout the whole world agrees in harmonious unanimity. For what commends our beloved Cornelius to God and to Christ and to his Church also commends him to all his fellow priests in praiseworthy commendation, namely that he did not come to the episcopacy suddenly, but was advanced through all the ecclesiastical offices: he often propitiated the Lord in the divine service and rose through all the ranks of religion to the exalted pinnacle of the priesthood. And furthermore, he neither asked for nor wanted the episcopacy itself, nor did he rush into it as others do, whom their swollen arrogance and pride make haughty. He is at other times gentle and forbearing, like those men usually are who are divinely chosen for this office. Because of the modesty arising from the continence he has always observed, and of the humility of his innate and well-guarded restraint, he did not bring about his ordination as bishop by violence, as some do, but he himself suffered violence to force him to accept the episcopacy. He was made a bishop by very many of our colleagues who were in the city of Rome at that time, and they sent us respectful and valuable letters about his ordination, marked by testimony given in praise of him. Cornelius was made a bishop by the judgment of God and his Christ, by the attestation of almost all the clerics, by the approbation of the people then present, by the body of older priests and good men. No one had been ordained before him; the place of Fabian[10]—that is, of

---

ˣText: CSEL 3,2,629-631.

[9]Bishop of Rome, 251-253; he was elected in preference to the rigorist Novatian, but Novatian claimed the see and wrote to Africa seeking support.

[10]Bishop of Rome, 236-250.

Peter—and the honor of the priestly chair were vacant. And since he filled them, and was confirmed by God's will and by the consent of all of us, any one who now wishes to be made bishop must do so outside; a man who does not preserve the unity of the Church cannot have an ecclesiastical ordination. Whoever he is, even if he makes as great a display of himself as possible, he is still secular, he is foreign, he is excluded. Since after the first bishop a second one is not possible, whoever is ordained after the one who ought to be the only one is not second but no bishop at all.

9. Thereupon, after he received the rank of bishop, not because he sought it or extorted it, but because he accepted it by the will of God, who makes priests, how much virtue did he exhibit in that episcopal office which he undertook, how much strength of soul, what solid faith! With simple hearts we should gaze deeply upon his virtues and praise them. Fearlessly he sat upon the priestly chair in Rome at that time when the hostile tyrant was threatening God's priests with all kinds of punishments. The emperor would have accepted the news that a rival prince had risen up against him more patiently and tolerantly than that a priest of God had been ordained for Rome. Beloved brother, shouldn't this man be extolled by the highest testimony of virtue and faith? Wouldn't he be counted among the glorious confessors and martyrs? For a long time he sat expecting those who would torture his body and avenge the raging tyrant. Cornelius resisted the deadly edicts and scorned their threats and tortures and torments. His opponents would have rushed upon him with a sword, or crucified him, or burned him in a fire, or torn apart his insides or his limbs with some other unheard-of kind of punishment. Even if the majesty and goodness of the Lord our protector, who willed to have this priest appointed, watched over him after his appointment, nevertheless Cornelius suffered whatever he could, as much as pertains to his devotion and fear, and first conquered by his priesthood the tyrant who was later defeated by the weapons of war.

10. But because some dishonest and nasty rumors are circulating about him, I do not want you to wonder, because you know that the work of the devil is always to wound God's servants with lies and to defame their resplendent reputations with wrong judgments, so that men, who in the light of their own consciences are pure, are soiled by outside gossip. You should know that our colleagues investigated the matter and found quite accurately that he was not stained or blemished by any certificate of sacrifice, as some are spreading about. Nor has he entered into unlawful communion with bishops who had sacrificed, but admitted to communion with us only those bishops whose case was heard and whose innocence was proved.

LETTER 67, 1-5

Cyprian and thirty-seven other bishops to the presbyter Felix and the congregations at Legio and Asturica, and to the Deacon Aelius and the people at Emerita.

1.[11]When we had come together, dearest brethren, we read the letter which you wrote to us through our fellow bishops Felix and Sabinus because of the integrity of your faith and your fear of God. You told us that Basilides and Martialis, who had been stained by certificates of idolatry and chained by the memory of their unspeakable crimes, ought not to exercise the episcopal office or carry out the priestly service of God. You wanted a decision on this question, and you wished to have your justified and quite necessary concern relieved either by the comfort or by the help of our judgment. But it is not so much our deliberations as the divine commandments which answer this request of yours. According to these commandments, a heavenly voice has already decreed, and God's law already prescribed, which and what sort of men should serve at the altar and celebrate the divine sacrifices. In Exodus God speaks to Moses and warns him, saying: "Let the priests who approach the Lord God be sanctified, lest the Lord perhaps desert them" [Exod 19:22]; and, "And when they approach

---

[11]Text: CSEL 3,2,735-740.

to serve at the altar of the Holy One, they will not bring sin upon themselves, lest they die" [Exod 30:20]. Likewise in Leviticus the Lord commands and says, "The man in whom there is stain and blemish will not approach to offer gifts to God" [Lev 21:17].

2. Since these things were predicted and manifested to us, our devotion must serve the divine precepts zealously. In matters of this sort the person may not be considered, nor may human indulgence credit anyone with anything, when the divinely written word intervenes and enacts a law. For we ought not to forget what the Lord said to the Jews through the prophet Isaiah; he rebuked them and was angry with them, because they disdained the divine precepts and followed human doctrines. "That people," he says, "honors me with their lips, but their hearts are far away from me. They worship me without reason, while they teach the commandments and doctrines of men" [Isa 29:13]. The Lord likewise repeats this in the gospel and says, "You reject God's commandment to establish your own tradition" [Mark 7:9]. We ought to have these words before our eyes, and think them over carefully and devoutly; for the ordination of priests we should choose only spotless and untainted leaders, who can offer the sacrifices to God in a holy and worthy manner and be heard in the prayers which they make for the safety of the Lord's people, since it is written: "God does not hear the sinner, but if a man worships God and does his will, him he hears" [John 9:31]. For this reason it is fitting that with complete diligence and under honest examination, those men be chosen for God's priesthood who clearly will be heard by God.

3. Nor should the people delude themselves into thinking that they can be immune from the contagion of this sin. They are in communion with a sinful priest and give their consent to the unjust and illicit episcopacy of their bishop. Through the prophet Hosea the divine judgment makes a threat and says: "Their sacrifices are like the bread of mourning; all who eat them will be contaminated" [Hos 9:4]; what he is teaching and showing is that all, without exception, who are profaned and contaminated by the sacri-

fice of an unjust priest are joined to his sin. We find this made clear in Numbers likewise, when Korah, Dathan and Abiram appropriate to themselves the right to offer sacrifice, against the priest Aaron. There too, the Lord commands through Moses that the people should be separated from them, lest they be joined to the criminals and themselves be drawn into the same guilt. "Separate yourselves," he says, "from the tents of hardened, unjust men, and do not touch anything which belongs to them, lest you also perish in their sin" [Num 16:26]. For this reason a congregation which is obedient to the Lord's precepts and fears God should separate itself from a sinful bishop and not participate in the sacrifices of a sacrilegious priest, especially since the congregation has the power both to elect worthy priests and to refuse unworthy ones.

4. We see this derived from divine authority: the priest is chosen in the presence of the people, under the eyes of all, and is approved as worthy and suitable by public judgment and testimony, as the Lord commands Moses in Numbers, saying: "Take Aaron your brother and Eleazar his son; and you will place them upon the mountain in the presence of the whole assembly. Strip Aaron of his stole and put it on Eleazar his son, and let Aaron lie down and die there"[Num 20:25-26]. God commands a priest to be appointed in the presence of the whole assembly: that is, he teaches and shows that priestly ordinations should be carried out only with the knowledge of the people and in their presence so that, with the congregation attending, the sins of wicked men may be discovered or the merits of good men be made known, and the ordination might be just and legitimate because it was pondered by the vote and the judgment of all. This was afterwards observed in the Acts of the Apostles according to the divine teachings, when Peter speaks to the people about ordaining a bishop in Judas's place. It says: "Peter rose up in the midst of the disciples, and the crowd was united" [Acts 1:15]. We notice that the apostles observed this not only for the ordinations of bishops and priests but also in the ordinations of deacons. On this very point there is a record in their Acts. It says: "And the Twelve called together the whole assembly of the disciples and said to them..." [Acts 6:2]. This choice was carried out so diligently and cautiously, with the whole congregation assembled, lest any unworthy person come by stealth to the service of the altar or to the priestly rank. For sometimes unworthy men are ordained, not according to God's will but according to human presumption. And that these appointments, which do not come from a legitimate and just ordination, are displeasing to God, God Himself makes clear through the prophet Hosea; he says: "They set up a king for themselves and not through me" [Hos 8:4].

5. For this reason, the practice which is observed by us and throughout almost all the provinces is to be observed and followed, a practice derived from divine tradition and apostolic observance, namely that to carry out ordinations properly, whichever bishops of the same province are nearest, gather with that congregation for which a bishop is to be ordained, and the bishop is chosen in the presence of the people, because they know the lives of individual candidates quite thoroughly, and have examined each one in his manner of living. We see this done among you in the ordination of our colleague Sabinus, so that by the vote of the whole brotherhood, and by the judgment of the bishops who had convened in your presence and those who had written to you about him, the episcopacy should be conferred upon him, and hands imposed on him to replace Basilides.

Nor can an ordination, once carried out rightly, be rescinded. Basilides, after his sins had been discovered and laid bare even by his own confession of guilt, went to Rome and deceived our colleague Stephen, who was far away and ignorant of the deed and of the truth. His intention was to seek to have himself restored unjustly to the episcopal office from which he was rightly deposed. This is relevant because Basilides' sins have not so much been abolished as increased in number, so that the crimes of intrigue and fraud have been added to his previous sins. Nor should we so much blame Stephen, who was taken unawares, as curse Basilides who defrauded and deceived him. Basilides might have been able to deceive men, but he cannot deceive God, since it is written: "God is not mocked" [Gal 6:7]. Nor can deception profit Martialis. He is immersed in serious sins and should not retain the episcopacy, since the Apostle gives warning and says: "The bishop, as God's steward, should be without sin" [Titus 1:7].

15. Ambrose of Milan

Ambrose was born in Trier (now in Germany) in the fourth decade of the fourth century. He was educated in rhetoric and law, and held the office of governor when, in 373 or 374, he was elected bishop of Milan. He had not yet been baptized, so that neither Arians nor Catholics could claim him. He remained bishop of Milan until his death in 397; his life was distinguished by his personal asceticism and his rigorous defense of the rights of the church. Letter 19, written in 385, gives advice to a young bishop, treating in particular the moral norms which Ambrose wants him to urge upon his congregation. In letter 63, which dates from about 396, Ambrose writes to the church at Vercelli, which had had the custom of electing a celibate ascetic as bishop. After the death of the most recent bishop, however, two former monks had caused a disturbance there by teaching that neither fasting nor virginity had any special merit, and urging the people to elect a married man as bishop. Ambrose urges the people of Vercelli to continue their custom and elect an ascetic as bishop. In the course of the letter, he compares the clerical state with the monastic life, showing his admiration for both, but his higher esteem of the former.

LETTER 19, 1-7
Ambrose to Vigilius.

1. [12] You sought from me the distinguishing marks of your appointed rank, because you are newly summoned to the

---

[12]Text: PL 16 (1880) 1024-1026.

priesthood. And since you, who have been judged worthy of this great office, prepared yourself for it appropriately, I should rightly tell you how to be of good service to others.

2. First of all recognize that the Lord's Church has been entrusted to you. Therefore you must always avoid having anything discrediting creep into it and have its body become a common thing by the addition of unbelievers. For this reason Scripture says to you, "Do not take a wife from the daughters of the Canaanites, but go into Mesopotamia, to the house of Bethuel (that is, to the house of wisdom), and make a bond with that house for yourself" [Gen 28:1-2]. Mesopotamia is a region in the area of the Orient which is enclosed by two great rivers which flow through those places, the Euphrates and the Tigris, whose source is in the regions of Armenia. By different courses they flow into the Red Sea; and thus the image of the Church is signified by the name Mesopotamia. The Church makes the hearts of the faithful fruitful by the abundant overflowing of the rivers of prudence and justice, for the Church bestows on the faithful the grace of sacred baptism, the type of which existed in the Red Sea, and washes away their sin. Therefore teach the people that they should seek the bond of marriage not with outsiders but from Christian households.

3. "Let no one defraud the day laborer of the wages owed him" [Lev 19:13], because we too are day laborers of our God, and we await from him the wages of our toil. And you, tradesman, whoever you are: you deny your laborer his monetary wages, which are something cheap and passing; but you will be denied the wages of the heavenly promises. As the Law says, "Therefore you will not defraud the day laborer of his wages" [Deut 24:14].

4. You shall not lend out your money at interest, because it is written that he who "did not lend out his money at interest will dwell in God's tabernacle" [Ps 15:1, 5], for he who derives profit from usury trips and falls. Therefore if a Christian man has money, he should give it out as if he did not expect to get it back, or at least to get back only the principal that he lent. In this transaction he reaps no small interest in grace. Otherwise, this is deceit rather than help, for what could be harsher than to give your money to

someone who has none and to demand twice as much back? If the man did not have enough to pay the sum once, how can he pay it twice?

5. Let Robit be an example to us. He never asked for money back which he had lent out except at the very end of his life; and then he did it to avoid defrauding his heir rather than to get back by force the money he lent. Nations have often perished because of interest due, and it is the cause of public calamity. Therefore it should be a special concern for us priests to trim off these vices, which we see creeping over so many people.

6. Teach that a guest should be received voluntarily rather than under duress, lest by postponing hospitality a man should produce an inhospitable inclination in his soul, and then when he does receive the guest, grace should suffer an injury. Hospitality should rather be cultivated by the habit of social obligation and by the ministrations of kindness. For it is not rich gifts that are asked of you, but voluntary service, filled with peace and with the harmony which accompanies it. For "vegetables served with friendliness and grace are better" [Prov 15:17] than a banquet adorned with exquisite dishes if a gracious attitude is lacking. We read that nations perished in terrible ruin because they violated the laws of hospitality, and on account of passion fearful wars have been waged.

7. But there is almost nothing more serious than marriage with a woman who is not a Christian, for there the motives of lust and discord are combined with the disgrace of sacrilege. Since the marriage bond itself should be sanctified by the priestly veiling and blessing, how can we speak of a bond where there is no agreement in the faith? Since their prayer should be made together, how can the common love of marriage exist between two who differ in their religion? It often happens; many men were enticed by the love of women and betrayed their faith, like the nation of our fathers at Beelphegor. For this reason Phinehas took a sword and slew the Hebrew man and the Midianite woman, and appeased the divine wrath, lest the whole nation be destroyed.

LETTER 63, 46. 61-66. 71-74.

Ambrose to the Church at Vercelli.

46. [13] Therefore, bad will should be absent from every action, but especially in the choice of a bishop, in whom the lives of all are regulated. In this acceptable and peaceable quality let the man who is chosen by all, and who can heal all, be preferred to all others. For "a gentle man is a physician of the soul" [Prov 14:30]. The Lord also called himself the physician of the soul in the gospel, when he said, "The healthy do not need a physician, but rather they who are ill" [Matt 9:12].

61. And so the Apostle supplied an ideal, that "a bishop ought to be irreprehensible" [1 Tim 3:2]. And he says elsewhere, "For a bishop, as God's steward, ought to be blameless, not proud, not irritable, not a drunkard, not a bandit, not desirous of ill-gotten wealth" [Titus 1:7]. For how can the mercy of a steward be reconciled with the avarice of a miser?

62. What I put down so far, I understand as wrongs to be avoided. But the Apostle is also a teacher of virtues. He teaches that opponents should be refuted patiently. He commands the bishop to be "the husband of one wife"[Titus 1:6], not in order to exclude a man who has never married (which goes beyond the law of precept) but so that the man might preserve the grace of his baptism in conjugal purity. Nor is he invited by apostolic authority to beget children as a priest, for Paul says a man who "has" children, not one who begets them or marries a second time.

63. I did not pass this point over, because many argue that "the husband of one wife" refers to a wife married after his baptism, because the guilt which creates the impediment is washed away by baptism.[14] All faults and sins are indeed washed away; if a man has defiled his body with very many

---

[13]Text: PL 16 (1880) 1253-1261.

[14]This was Jerome's view; see his *Letter* 69.

women, but has not bound them to himself by the law of marriage, all is forgiven him. But if a man has married a second or third time, the bonds are not dissolved, because baptism dissolves guilt, but it does not dissolve the law. What is legally binding, therefore, is not remitted, as if it were guilty; it still holds, because it is law. And the Apostle formulated a law, saying: "If a man is without guilt, the husband of one wife" [Titus 1:6]. Therefore a man who is blameless, the husband of one wife, is qualified under the law to receive the priesthood; a man who married a second time is not guilty of defilement, but is deprived of the privilege of a priest.

64. We have stated what belongs to law; let us also speak from reason. But let us first recognize that not only did the Apostle prescribe this for the bishop and the presbyter, but the fathers in consultation at the Nicene Council added that no one who had entered a second marriage should be a cleric. For how could he console a widow, honor her, urge her to preserve her widowhood and remain faithful to her husband, if he did not respect his first marriage? Or what difference is there between people and priest, if they are bound by the same laws? The priest's life ought to surpass the layman's, just as his grace does; for whoever binds others by his commands ought himself to observe legitimate commandments.

65. How I resisted being ordained! When I was finally forced to accept it, I wished that it might at least be postponed. But the law did not allow it, and pressure won the day. Nevertheless the western bishops approved of my ordination in a formal judgment, the eastern bishops by their example, despite the fact that a neophyte may not be ordained lest his pride be fed. If my ordination lacked the proper waiting time, it was due to the power of force. If the humility proper to the priestly office is not wanting, guilt will not be imputed without a cogent reason.

66. But if so much though is given to choosing a bishop in other churches, how much care is needed in the church of Vercelli, where two demands are made of the bishop, the continence of monastic life and the government of the church? Eusebius, of blessed memory, was the first one in the West to unite these two different disciplines; while living in the city he observed the monastic way of life, and he governed the church while keeping a sober fast. Much profit accrues to the grace of a priest if the bishop disciplines the young clergy in the practice of abstinence and in the rule of purity and if he forbids them the practices of the city and its way of life even though they live in the city.

71. This endurance grew strong in the holy Eusebius through the practices of the monastery, and from growing accustomed to a more severe way of life he drew the ability to endure hardship. For who doubts that for more fully dedicated Christians these two states of life are more excellent, namely the ranks of the clergy and the way of life of monks? The clerical state teaches forbearance and good character, the monastic life accustoms a man to abstinence and endurance. The cleric lives almost in a theater, the monk in hiding; the one is observed, the other hidden. Thus the good athlete says, "We have been made a spectacle to this world and to angels"[1 Cor 4:9]. Certainly the man who is observed by angels is worthy to receive Christ's reward for victory after his struggle; and while he is struggling to establish the life of angels on earth, he is worthy to repair the sin of the angels in heaven, for he is struggling against spiritual evils. The world is right to observe him, in order to imitate him.

72. The one way of life is lived in a race course, the other in a cave. The cleric opposes the disorder of the world, the monk the appetite of the flesh; one tames the body's pleasures, the other flees from them. The cleric's life is more pleasant, the monk's safer; the cleric moderates his life, the monk restrains it. Yet each denies himself, that Christ may flourish, because it is said to the perfect, "Whoever wishes to come after me must deny himself and take up his cross and follow me"[Matt 16:24]. So the man who can say "I live, but now not I, but Christ lives in me" [Gal 2:20] is following Christ.

73. Paul denied himself when, knowing that chains and

torments awaited him in Jerusalem, he freely exposed himself to dangers, saying, "I do not consider my life of value to me, so long as I can accomplish my journey and the ministry of the word which I received from the Lord Jesus" [Acts 20:24]. Many people stood around him, weeping and imploring him, but he did not turn his heart back. Courageous faith passes harsh judgment on itself.

74. The cleric struggles, the monk withdraws. The one defeats allurements, the other escapes them. The one triumphs over the world, the other is an exile from the world. The world is crucified to the cleric, and he to the world; the monk ignores the world. The cleric has many temptations, and therefore the greater victory; the monk falls less frequently, and can guard himself more easily.

16. Jerome

Jerome is best known for his work in translating the Bible and commenting on it, and almost as well know for his contentiousness and severity. He was born ca. 347, in Stridon in Dalmatia (now Yugoslavia), and died in 419 or 420 in Bethlehem. After a good education he tried for several years to live in the East as a monk. He returned to Rome in 382, becoming secretary to Pope Damasus and adviser to some wealthy women who had taken up an ascetical life. His departure from Rome in 385 was sudden and unpleasant; he spent the rest of his life in a primitive monastery in Bethlehem. Excerpts from three of his letters are included here. Jerome wrote letter 14 in 373 or 374 to his friend Heliodorus, who gave up the ascetical life and lived as a cleric; in the passage translated here, Jerome compares the two states. Letter 52 was addressed in 394 to the presbyter Nepotian, the nephew of Heliodorus (who was now a bishop). Jerome proposes a severe style of life for this priest-monk and includes biting satires of clerical faults. In letter 146 Jerome explains to Evangelus that in the early Church "bishop" and "presbyter" were two names for the same office, and illustrates this from the New Testament.

LETTER 14, 8-9

To the Monk Heliodorus.

8. [15] Once you have been driven from this position [that a monk can be perfect in his own country], you will appeal to the clerics: "Can I dare to say anything about these men, who certainly dwell in their cities?" I shun saying anything unfavorable about them, since they succeed to the apostolic rank and confect the body of Christ with their holy mouths. It is through them that we too are Christians; they hold the keys of the kingdom of heaven. In a certain way they judge before the day of judgment, since they preserve the Lord's bride in sober chastity. But as I have already argued, the situation of a monk is one thing, that of clerics another. (2) Clerics pasture the sheep, I am pastured. They live from the altar; I am like a sterile tree, and the axe is laid to my roots, if I do not bring my gift to the altar. Nor can I offer poverty as an excuse, when I see the old woman in the gospel casting in two bronze coins, which was all she had left. I may not sit in the presence of a presbyter; if I sin, he may hand me over to Satan for the destruction of the flesh, so that the spirit might be saved. (3) And in the Old Law, whoever did not obey the priests was either taken outside the camp and stoned by the people or paid in blood for his scorn with his neck laid under the sword. But now the disobedient man is cut down by a spiritual sword, or expelled from the church and torn to pieces by the savage mouths of demons. (4) If the devout flattery of the brethren tempts you also to this rank, I will rejoice in your rise and I will fear for your fall. "The man who desires the episcopacy desires a good work" [1 Tim 3:1]. We know these words, but add what follows: "But this sort of man should be blameless, the husband of one wife, sober,

[15] Text: CSEL 54.55-59, ed. by I. Hilberg (1910).

chaste, prudent, distinguished, hospitable, teachable, not a drunkard, not violent, but modest" [1 Tim 3:2-3]. (5) And after he set forth the rest of the qualifications of the bishop, which follow, he prescribed no less caution for the third rank: "Deacons likewise should be modest, not two-faced, not given to much wine, not making profits dishonestly, keeping the mystery of the faith in a clean conscience; and let them be tested first and thus, without any fault, let them serve" [1 Tim 3:8-10]. (6) Woe to that man who goes in to the supper but has no wedding garment! The only possibility is that he will immediately hear this: "Friend, how did you enter here?" [Matt 22:12]. He will fall silent and the servants will be told, "Take him up by the feet and hands and throw him into the darkness outside; there there will be weeping and gnashing of teeth" [Matt 22:13]. (7) Woe to that man who received a talent and bound it up in a handkerchief, so that while the others were making profits he merely kept what he had received! He will be struck on the spot by the shout of the indignant master: "Useless servant, why didn't you give my money to a money-changer? I could have come and demanded it back with interest" [Luke 19:22-23]. That is: "You placed at the altar what you could not carry. And while you, you lazy trader, hold on to your denarius, you have taken the place of another man who could have doubled the money." For this reason, just as the man who serves well acquires a good rank for himself, so the one who approaches the Lord's chalice unworthily will be guilty of the Lord's body and blood.

9. Not all bishops are good bishops. You think of Peter, but consider Judas, too. You look up to Stephen, but think also of Nicolaus, whom the Lord hates in his Apocalypse.[16] He contrived such vile and heinous errors that the heresy of the Ophites grew out of that root. Each one should first examine himself and thus come forward. Ecclesiastical rank does not make a Christian. While he was still a pagan, the centurion Cornelius was deluged with the gift of the Holy

---

[16]The Fathers often identified the Nicolaus of Acts 6:5, one of the Seven, with the founder of the heretical Nicolaitans of Apoc 2, 6. 15.

Spirit. As a boy, Daniel passes judgment on presbyters. Amos is suddenly made a prophet while picking blackberries. The shepherd David is chosen as king. Jesus loves the least disciple the most. (2) Brother, take the lower place, so that when a less important person comes along you may be asked to go higher. Upon whom will the Lord come to rest, except upon one who is humble and silent and respects his words? More will be demanded of the man to whom more is entrusted. "The mighty will suffer mightily in torment"[Wis 6:6]. Nor should anyone congratulate himself merely on the chastity of a pure body, since on the day of judgment men are going to have to render an account of every idle word that they ever spoke, when even a man who shouts at his brother will be guilty of murder. (3) It is not easy to stand in Paul's place, to hold the rank of those who already reign with Christ; an angel might come, split the veil of your temple, and remove your candlestick from its place. If you are planning to build a tower reckon up the cost of the work to be done. Tasteless salt is good for nothing else but to be thrown outside and trodden on by the swine. If a monk falls, the priest will intercede for him; who will intercede for a fallen priest?

LETTER 52, 5-17

To Nepotian.

5.[17] So let the cleric, who serves Christ's Church, first appreciate his name; and once his name has been defined, let him strive to be what he is called. For if the Greek word *klēros* means "portion," clerics are called this either because they belong to the Lord's portion or because the Lord himself is the portion, that is, the share, for clerics. (2) The man who possesses the Lord and says with the prophet, "The Lord is my portion" [Ps 73:26] can have nothing besides the Lord because, if he does have anything else besides the Lord, the Lord will not be his portion. For

[17]Text: CSEL 54.421-441.

example, if he has gold, or silver, or estates, or inlaid furniture, the Lord does not deign to become his portion along with these portions. But if I am the Lord's portion and the cord of his inheritance and I do not receive a portion with the rest of the tribes, but like a Levite and a priest I live from the tithes and am sustained by the offerings on the altar as I serve the altar, I have food and clothing and will be content with these; naked I will follow the naked cross. (3) And so I beseech you, "and going back I will warn you again and again"[18] not to think that the clerical office is like your former military service—that is, do not seek worldly profit in Christ's service. You should not possess more than you did when you began to be a cleric, and you were told: "Their portions will not profit them" [Jer 12:13,]. Let the poor and the strangers, and with them Christ, come to your table as guests. Avoid the clerical businessman, the pauper become rich and the ostentatious former commoner, as you would some plague. "Bad conversations corrupt good morals" [1 Cor 15:33].

(4) You despise gold, another loves it; you tread on wealth, he pursues it. You love silence, gentleness and solitude; he loves much talk, a shameless brow, public places, city streets and physicians' taverns. With such a difference in morals what agreement can exist? Women's feet should seldom or never tread the floor of your little house. Either ignore equally all young women and virgins dedicated to Christ, or love them equally. Do not live in the same house with them. Do not trust in your past chastity. You cannot be holier than David or wiser than Solomon. Always remember that a woman ejected the dweller in paradise from his portion. (5) If you are sick let some holy brother help you, or a sister or mother, or another woman whose faith is approved by all. But if there are no women who are thus related to you and modest, the church supports many old women who offer this help and profit by serving, so that your sickness can bear fruit in almsgiving. I know some clerics who regained their bodily health and began to be ill

---

[18]Vergil. *Aeneid* 3. 436.

spiritually. If you pay frequent attention to a woman's face, it is dangerous for her to serve you. (6) If you have to visit a widow or a virgin in the course of your clerical duties, never enter the house alone, but bring companions with you whose company will not harm your reputation. If a reader, acolyte or cantor accompanies you, he should be distinguished by his manners rather than his clothing. They should not crimp their hair with a curling iron; their dress should bespeak modesty. Do not sit alone with a woman privately and without a witness. If she has to speak of something more personal, she has a nurse, or a virgin housekeeper, or a widow or a married woman; she is not so unsocial that she has no one but you to whom she dares entrust herself. (7) Beware of all suspicions and preclude having people imagine what perhaps they might. Holy love has no place for numerous little gifts, and dainty handkerchiefs, and garters, and garments pressed to the lips, and foods tasted delicately and sweet enticing notes. In comedies, we blush at "my sweetness, my light, and my desire," and the rest of lovers' absurdities, all of them allurements, and charms and ridiculous pleasantries. We detest them in men of the world; how much more in clerics and clerical monks, whose priesthood is enhanced by their monastic vocation and their monastic vocation by their priesthood! (8) I do not say this because I fear these errors in you or in holy men, but because in every way of life, in every rank and both sexes, both good and evil people are found, and the condemnation of the evil is the praise of the good.

6. I am ashamed to say it, but the priests of idols, actors of mimes, charioteers, and prostitutes may receive inheritances; to clerics and monks alone is this forbidden by law—and forbidden not by persecutors but by Christian princes.[19] I do not complain about the law, but I grieve because we deserved this law. Cautery is good, but where did I get the wound that needs cautery? The legal precaution is prudent

---

[19] An imperial letter of 370 to Pope Damasus forbade clerics to solicit or receive legacies from widows or orphans; English translation in P. R. Coleman-Norton, *Roman State and Christian Church* I (London, 1966), 326.

and strict, but avarice is still not restrained. (2) We ridicule
the law by bequests given to a third person for us, and, as if
the emperors' decrees were greater than Christ's, we fear the
laws and despise the gospels. Let there be an heir, but let it
be the church, the mother of the children—her flock—for
she bore, nourished and supported them. Why do we place
ourselves between the mother and the children? The glory of
a bishop is to provide for the support of the poor; the
disgrace of all priests is to care for their own wealth. (3) I was
born in a poor house, in a country hut, and was hardly able
to fill my growling stomach with millet bread or black
bread. Now I scorn the finest wheat flour and honey; I know
the kinds and names of fish; I have learned how to tell what
shore a mussel was gathered from; I distinguish the provinces that birds come from by their taste; the rarity of foods
and recently the very cost delight me. (4) I also hear of the
vile subservience of some to old men and women without
children. They themselves hold the chamber pot; they
occupy the bedside and receive the foul discharge of the
stomach or phlegm from the lungs in their own hands. They
are terrified at the arrival of the doctor and they ask with
trembling lips whether the patients are more comfortable
and, if the old person gets a little stronger, they are threatened; they put on a show of happiness, but their greedy
hearts are secretly tortured, (5) for they fear that their
services have gone to waste and that the sprightly old man
will live as long as Methuselah. How great a reward they
would have from the Lord, if they did not hope for payment
in this life! How much sweat is expended on an empty
legacy! The pearl of Christ could be bought with less work!

7. Read the divine Scriptures often—rather, never let the
sacred page drop from your hands. Learn what you should
teach. Preserve that faithful word, which adheres to the
teaching, so that you may teach sound doctrine and refute
those who oppose you: "Abide in what you have learned,
and what has been entrusted to you, knowing by whom you
were taught" [2 Tim 3:14]. Always be ready to give a satis-
factory account to all who ask of that hope which is in you.
(2) Your actions may not contradict your teaching lest,

when you speak in church, someone might answer you silently, "Why, therefore, do you not do this yourself?" It is a dainty teacher who can discourse about fasting on a full stomach. Even a thief can accuse someone of avarice. The thoughts and words of a priest of Christ should agree. Be submissive to your bishop and look to him as the father of your soul. Sons love; slaves fear. "And if I am the father," it says, "where is my honor? And if I am the Lord, where is the reverence due me?" [Mal 1, 6]. (3) You must respect several titles in the same man: monk, bishop, uncle. But the bishops too should realize that they are priests, not masters; let them honor the clerics as clerics, just as the clerics show deference to them as bishops. This is the law of the orator Domitius: "Should I," he said, "treat you as a ruler, when you do not treat me as a senator?"[20] What we know of Aaron and his sons applies to the bishop and the presbyters: let there be one lord, one temple, one ministry. (4) We should always be mindful of what the apostle Peter teaches priests: "Feed the Lord's flock which is with you with care; not by force but freely according to God; nor for the sake of foul profit but voluntarily; nor as if you were lording it over the clergy but willingly being a model for the flock, so that when the prince of pastors appears you may receive the imperishable crown of glory" [1 Pet 5:2-4]. (5) There is a bad custom in some churches, whereby the presbyters remain silent and do not speak when bishops are present, as if they either were jealous or do not deign to listen. The apostle Paul says, "And if something is revealed to another, who is sitting, let the first one be silent. For you can prophesy one by one, so that all learn and all are consoled. And the spirit of prophets is subject to prophets, for God is not the God of dissension but of peace" [1 Cor 14:30-33]. The father's glory is a wise son; let the bishop rejoice in his judgment, when he chooses such priests for Christ.

8. When you speak in the church, you should not arouse the people's applause but their groans. The tears of your listeners should be your praise. Let the presbyter's preach-

---

[20]Cicero, *De oratore* 3, 1.

ing be based on his reading of the Scriptures. I do not want you to be a declaimer, or argumentative, or long-winded, but experienced in the mystery and most learned in the sacraments of your God. To pour out words and to arouse admiration among the inexperienced crowd by the swiftness of one's speech is typical of unschooled men. Such a one often shamelessly explains what he does not know and, when he has convinced others, convinces himself too. (2) Once I asked my onetime teacher Gregory of Nazianzus to explain what the *deuteroproton* (that is, the "secondfirst") Sabbath means in Luke [Luke 6:1]. He made a fine joke and said, "I will teach you about this matter in the church, where with the whole people applauding for me you will be forced unwillingly to know what you are ignorant of—or surely, if you alone are silent, you alone will be accused of stupidity by all." Nothing is easier than deceiving a simple congregation or an uneducated assembly with a fluent tongue; whatever they do not understand they admire all the more. Listen to what Marcus Tullius—to whom this beautiful tribute applies, "Demosthenes prevented you from being the first orator, but you prevented him from being the only one"— says in his speech for Quintus Gallius about the favor of a crowd and unskilled orators: "But one particular poet—for I speak of what I myself have recently witnessed— dominates these contests, a very learned man, who writes of the banquets of poets and philosophers. He makes Euripides and Menander carry on a conversation, or elsewhere Socrates and Euripides, although we know that their lifetimes differed not by years but by centuries. What great applause and shouting he gets by these compositions! For he has many fellow disciples in the theater; they too never learned any literature."

9. Avoid both somber and gaudy clothing. Shun adornment and squalor equally; the one reeks of delicacy, the other of vanity. Not to be able to afford linen garments is praiseworthy. Otherwise it is ridiculous and quite dishonest to have a purse stuffed with money and boast that you have no handkerchief or towel. (2) There are people who give a little money to the poor in order to receive more; under the

pretense of almsgiving, they seek riches. This should be called hunting rather than almsgiving; this is the way animals, birds and fish are caught. A little bit of food is placed on the hook so that noble women's purses can be reeled in on it. The bishop, to whom the church is entrusted, knows whom to put in charge of caring for the poor and giving them help. It is better to have nothing to give than to ask shamelessly. (3) To wish to appear more generous than the bishop is also a kind of arrogance. "Not all of us can do everything."[21] In the church one person is an eye, another the tongue, another a hand, another a foot, another an ear, the stomach, and so on. Read Paul's letters to the Corinthians: different members make up one body. The brother who is only a simple peasant should not consider himself holy merely because he is ignorant; nor should the learned and eloquent man claim sanctity. Of the two imperfect possibilities, a holy peasant is much better than a sinful scholar.

10. Many construct walls and haul columns to the church. Marble gleams, the panelled ceilings glisten with gold, the altar is adorned with jewels; yet there is no care in choosing the ministers of Christ. And no one should object that there was in Judea a rich temple, a table, lamps, censers, plates, cups, mortars and other objects crafted out of gold. (2) These objects were approved by the Lord at the time when priests slaughtered victims and the blood of cattle redeemed from sin—although all these things were first given in types; "They have been written for our sake, upon whom the ends of the ages have come"[1 Cor 10:11]. But now, since a poor Lord has hallowed the poverty of His house, we should contemplate the cross and judge that riches are slime. Why do we admire money, which Christ called evil? Why do we admire and love what Peter said he had none of? (3) Otherwise, if we follow the letter only and a simple story of gold and riches delights us, let us observe the rest of the laws along with this gold. Let the priests of Christ marry virgins as wives. Let a man who has a scar and is deformed be deprived of the priesthood, even though he has a right

---

[21]Vergil, *Eclogues* 8, 63.

intention. Let corporeal leprosy, rather than spiritual vices, be the criterion. Let us increase and multiply and fill the earth. Let us not sacrifice the Lamb or celebrate the mystical Pasch, because these acts are forbidden by the Law apart from the temple. Let us build a shelter in the seventh month, and let us sound a solemn fast on the trumpet. But if we understand all these laws by comparing spiritual things with other spiritual things, knowing with Paul that the law is spiritual, and singing David's words, "Open my eyes and I will contemplate the wonders of your law" [Ps 119:18] just as our Lord understood and interpreted the Sabbath, we should either repudiate gold along with the rest of the Jews' superstitions or, if we are pleased by gold, the Jews should also please us. Either we have to approve of them along with gold or reject both.

11. You should avoid the banquets of secular people, and especially of those who proudly boast of their distinctions. It is disgraceful to see consuls' lictors and bodyguards lounging before the door of a priest of the crucified and poor Lord who was fed with another's bread; it is equally disgraceful for a provincial judge to eat better at your table than in his palace. (2) You may object that you do this to beg for the unfortunate and the downtrodden. A civil judge defers more to a continent cleric than to a rich one, and respects your holiness more than your money—or, if he is the kind of man who will not listen to clerics except over a wine cup, I will be happy to do without this sort of charity, and will pray to Christ for that judge, because Christ is better able to help. "It is better to trust in the Lord than to trust in man, better to hope in the Lord than to hope in princes" [Ps 118:8-9]. (3) See that you never smell of wine, lest you hear that philosopher's saying, "This kiss isn't given, it's poured." The Apostle condemns drunken priests, and the Old Law forbids those who serve at the altar to drink wine or *sicera*.[22] In the Hebrew language *sicera* means every drink which can inebriate, whether it is made from

---

[22]Greek and Latin form of the Hebrew *shechar*, usually translated "strong drink"; found at Lev 10:9 and Luke 1:15.

yeast or the juice of apples, or honeycombs are boiled down into a sweet and barbaric drink, or the fruits of palm trees are pressed for their juice, or a rich liquid is strained from cooked grain. Avoid whatever inebriates and upsets the mind's balance, just as you avoid wine. (4) I do not mean that a creature of God is condemned by us, if—as is true—the Lord was called a wine-drinker and a moderate drink of wine soothed Timothy's stomach ailment; but we do in drinking take into account the bounds of age, and health, and the qualities of the body. If I am passionate without wine, if I am passionate with youth, if I am inflamed with the heat of my blood and have a vigorous and strong body, I will gladly do without the wine cup, which contains the suspicion of poison. The Greeks have an elegant saying, but I don't know whether it sounds as good in our language: "A fat belly doesn't foster refined taste."

12. Impose only as much fasting on yourself as you can tolerate. Your fasts should be pure, chaste, simple and moderate, not superstitious. What profit is there in not eating oil but creating annoyance and difficulties in getting food? The entire growth of the gardens is strained: we seek dried figs, pepper, nuts, dates, wheat flour, honey, and pistachio nuts, because we are fasting from ordinary bread. Moreover, I also hear that some people, against the natural order and human nature, do not drink water or eat bread, but drink tiny little sips of pressed vegetables and beet juice, and that not from a cup but from a sea shell. It is a disgrace that we are not embarrassed by this sort of absurdity, and do not find this superstition disgusting! We even seek a reputation for abstinence while eating these delicacies. The best fast of all is bread and water. But since this is not glorious and all of us live on bread and water, it is not considered a fast because it is public and usual.

13. Beware of lying in wait for men's gossip, lest you pay for people's praise with God's disfavor. The Apostle says, "If I were still pleasing to men, I would not be Christ's servant" [Gal 1:10]. He ceased pleasing men and became a servant of Christ. The soldier of Christ makes progress through good reputation and bad, on the right and on the

left; he is not inflated by praise or crushed by censure; he is
not swollen up by riches or shrivelled by poverty; he condemns both joy and sorrow. By day the sun does not burn
him, nor the moon by night. (2) I do not want you to pray on
the street corners, lest the air of popularity deflect the
straight path of your prayers. I do not want you to widen
your fringes, to have phylacteries to show off, and to be
absorbed by pharisaical ambition as your conscience fights
back. It is better to carry these things in your heart than on
your body, to have God as your advocate rather than men's
eyes. Do you wish to know what sort of adornment the Lord
seeks? Have prudence, justice, temperance, fortitude. (3) Be
bound by these regions of heaven, let this team of four stir
you up and bring you like Christ's charioteer to the goal
post. Nothing is more precious than this necklace, nothing
more distinguished than this array of jewels. You are
adorned, girded and protected on every side; these virtues
are your ornaments and your protection; jewels are turned
into shields.

14. Beware too of having a tongue or ears that itch: that is,
do not defame others or listen to people who defame others.
Scripture says, "You sat and spoke against your brother and
you placed a stumbling block for your mother's son; you did
this and I was silent. You plotted evil, and I will be like you. I
will reprove you, and pass judgment before your face" [Ps
50:20-21]—we can add: "Upon your discourses and upon
everything which you said about other people. When you
are convicted of those things that you charged others with,
you are condemned by your own verdict." (2) Nor is this
excuse justified, that "I cannot insult others who tell me
something." No one likes to tell something to an unwilling
listener. An arrow is never fixed in a stone; it bounces back
and strikes the one who shot it. When he sees that you do not
listen willingly, the detractor should learn that he should not
easily defame another. Solomon says, "Do not associate
with detractors, because their destruction will come suddenly, and who knows the ruin of both?" [Prov 24:21-22]—
that is, the destruction of the detractor as well as of him who
attunes his ear to the detractor.

15. It belongs to your office to visit the sick, to know their households, and the married women and their children, and not to disregard the secrets of distinguished men. Therefore it belongs to your office to keep not only your eyes guarded, but also your tongue. Never discuss women's beauty. One household should not learn through you what is happening in another. (2) Before he would teach, Hippocrates bound his pupils by an oath and forced them to swear in his words. By an oath he made them keep silence; he prescribed their speech, their gait, their dress and their habits. How much more should we, to whom the care of souls is entrusted, love the homes of all Christians as if they were our own! They should know us rather as consolers in grief than as companions in good times. A cleric who is often invited to dinner and does not refuse is easily despised.

16. We should never seek a favor, and rarely accept if we are asked to receive one. In some unknown way even a man who begs to give you something respects you less when you accept it, and remarkably admires you more if you refuse him when he asks. As a preacher of continence, do not arrange marriages. Why does a man who reads the Apostle force a virgin to marry? For he writes, "It remains to say that those who have wives should act as if they did not have them" [1 Cor 7:29]. Why should a man who is a priest on the condition that he married only once urge a widow to marry a second time? (2) How can those who are bidden to despise their own property be the administrators or managers of others' houses and villas? To take something from a friend is theft; to deceive the church is sacrilege. If you have received a gift to be distributed to the poor and the many who are starving, and you want to be cautious or hesitant or—what is most clearly sinful—to take some part of the gift for yourself, you surpass every thief in cruelty. (3) I am tortured by hunger and you judge how much food will fill my stomach? Either pass out immediately what you have received, or, if you are a timid steward, tell the donor to distribute his gifts himself. I do not want to be the reason why your purse is full. No one can guard my possessions better than I. The best steward is one who keeps nothing for himself.

17. You have forced me, my dearest Nepotian, after ten years in Bethlehem to open my mouth again and to subject myself to the tongues of all who attack me. The little book on virginity[23] which I had written for the holy Eustochium at Rome has already been assailed. Either I should not have written anything, so that I would not be subjected to men's judgment—but you would not let me do that—or I should write knowing that the weapons of all who slander me would be turned against me. I beg them to be silent and to cease abusing me; we did not write as adversaries but as friends. Nor do we attack those who sin, but urge them not to sin. We were harsh judges not only against them, but against ourselves, too, and we cast the timber out of our own eye before we tried to remove the speck from another's eye. I injured no one; at least no one's identity was revealed by a description; my discourse did not strike out at anyone in particular. The discourse about errors is in general terms. The man who wants to be angry with me should first admit that he fits my description.

LETTER 146

To the Presbyter Evangelus.

1.[24] We read in Isaiah, "The fool will say foolish things" [Isa 32:6]. I hear that one man has broken out into such folly that he puts deacons before presbyters, that is, before bishops. Since the Apostle clearly teaches that presbyters are the same as bishops, what is this server of tables and widows suffering from, that he arrogantly exalts himself above those at whose prayers the body and blood of Christ are confected? Do you want an authority? Listen to this testimony: "Paul and Timothy, servants of Christ Jesus, to all the saints in Christ Jesus who are in Philippi, along with the bishops and deacons" [Phil 1:1]. (2) Do you want another example, too? In the Acts of the Apostles Paul

---

[23]Jerome's *Letter* 22.

[24]Text: CSEL 56.308-312, ed. by I. Hiberg

speaks thus to the priests of one church: "Attend to your-selves and the whole flock, in which the Holy Spirit has appointed you bishops, to rule the Lord's church which he won by his blood" [Acts 20:28]. (3) And lest anyone argue contentiously that there were several bishops in one church, hear another testimony also, which proves absolutely clearly that bishop and presbyter are the same: "I left you on Crete for this reason, to correct what was wrong and to establish presbyters in the cities, as I commanded you, if anyone is blameless, the husband of one wife, and has children who are believers, free from suspicion of extravan-gance and not unsubmissive. For a bishop, as God's ste-ward, should be blameless" [Titus 1:5-7]. (4) And to Timothy: "Do not neglect the grace of prophecy which has been given to you through the imposition of hands of the presbyterate" [1 Tim 4:14]. And Peter, too, in his first letter, says: "I beg the presbyters among you, I, your fellow presby-ter and witness of Christ's sufferings and future glory, which is to be revealed: I beg you to rule Christ's flock and to oversee them not by force but freely, according to God" [1 Pet 5:1-2]. The Greek word here for "oversee" is more meaningful: it is *episkopeuontes*, from which the name "bishop" is derived. (5) Do the testimonies of such great men seem insignificant to you? The son of thunder whom Jesus loved the most and who drank the rivers of instruction from the Savior's breast sounds a blast on the gospel trumpet: "The presbyter to the elect lady and her children, whom I love in the truth" [2 John 1:1], and in another letter, "The presbyter to dearest Gaius, whom I love in the truth" [3 John 1:1]. The fact that afterwards one was chosen who was placed above the others was done as a remedy for schism, to avoid having each one draw a following to himself and break up Christ's Church. (6) For at Alexandria from Mark the Evangelist up to the bishops Heraclas and Dionysius the presbyters always chose one of their number, placed him in the higher rank and named him bishop,[25] in the way in

[25]On the ordination of the bishop of Alexandria by presbyters see W. Telfei, "Episcopal Succession in Egypt," *Journal of Ecclesiastical History* 3 (1952), 1-13.

which the army makes an emperor or the deacons choose one of their own number whose dedication they recognize and call him "archdeacon." For, with the exception of ordinations, what does a bishop do that a presbyter does not do? The church of the City of Rome should not be judged by one standard, the rest of the world by another. (7) Gaul, Britain, Africa, Persia, the Orient, India, and all the barbarian nations adore one Christ and observe one norm of the truth. If authority is sought, the world is bigger than the City. Wherever there is a bishop, whether at Rome or Gubbio, at Constantinople or Reggio, at Alexandria or Tanis, he has the same worth and the same priesthood. The power of riches and the humility of poverty make a bishop higher or lower; in every other way they are all successors of the apostles.

2. But you will say: "How is it that at Rome a presbyter is ordained at the attestation of a deacon?" Why do you bring me the custom of one city? Why do you lay claim to the exception for the laws of the church? The exception is the source of pride. Everything that is rare is more sought after; among Indians, pennyroyal is more precious than pepper. Their small number makes the deacons honorable; the crowd of presbyters is held in contempt. But even in the church of Rome the presbyters sit and the deacons stand, although as errors gradually become more common I did see a deacon sitting among the presbyters when the bishop was absent, and giving blessings to presbyters at household celebrations. (2) Those who do this should learn that they are not acting rightly and should listen to the apostles: "It is not proper for us to leave God's word to serve tables" [Acts 6:2]. Let them realize why deacons were instituted; let them read the Acts of the Apostles and be mindful of their place. With "presbyter" and "bishop," the first word designates age, the second designates rank. Therefore in the letters to Timothy and to Titus the ordinations of a bishop and a deacon are treated, but concerning presbyters there is silence, because the presbyter is contained in the bishop. A man who is promoted goes from the lesser to the greater. Therefore either let a presbyter be ordained deacon, to prove that a presbyter is inferior to a deacon, since he grows

into this rank from a low one, or, if the deacon is ordained presbyter, let him recognize that the presbyter has a smaller income but is greater in the priesthood. And that we might realize that the apostolic traditions are drawn from the Old Testament, the fact that Aaron and his sons and the Levites were in the temple should justify the presence of bishops and presbyters and deacons in the church.

17. Augustine of Hippo
Sermon 355

Augustine was without a doubt the greatest theologian of the early Church; either the *Confessions*, or the *City of God*, or *On the Trinity* alone would have assured his reputation. But he wrote all of these and much more. Perhaps his most lasting achievement is his doctrine of grace. He was born in 354 in Thagaste (North Africa), baptized in Milan in 387 by Ambrose, and ordained bishop at Hippo Regius in Africa in 396. He died in 430. The sermon translated here shows an aspect of Augustine that is less frequently seen: Augustine the pastor of a church. Augustine had wanted his clergy to live with him in the bishop's house in monastic style, and to hold all their property in common. As the sermon shows, this was unsuccessful. One of his priests, on his deathbed, had made a will and thus claimed the right to dispose of property as his own. This scandal threatened the good name of Augustine's community, and disappointed him bitterly. Augustine here abandons his requirement of personal poverty and life in common for his clergy.

The[26] fifteenth day before the Kalends of January, Theodosius Augustus for the eleventh time and Valentinian Caesar for the first time, consuls.[27]

[26]Text: *Sermones Selecti*, ed. by C. Lambot (Utreet and Brussels, 1950), 124-131.
[27]That is, 18 December, 425.

1. Yesterday I wanted and asked you to assemble today in larger numbers for this reason—namely, what I am going to say. We live here with you, and we live here for you. It is our intention and our desire to live with you forever in Christ's company. I am also convinced that our way of life is known to you, so that we could also perhaps dare to say (although we are hardly his equals) what the Apostle said: "Be imitators of me, as I am of Christ" [1 Cor 4:16]. And therefore I do not want any one of you to find an excuse for bad living. The Apostle also says, "We intend good, not only before God but also before men" [2 Cor 8:21]. As far as we are concerned, our clear conscience is enough for us. As far as you are concerned, our good name should not be dishonored but respected by you. Remember what I said, but make a distinction. Conscience and a good name are two different things. Conscience is yours; your good name is your neighbor's. One who trusts in his conscience and neglects his good name is cruel, especially if he holds that place of which the Apostle says, as he writes to his disciple, "Offer yourself as an example of good works to all" [Titus 2:7].

2. So as not to keep you too long, especially because I am sitting as I speak, but you are burdened with standing: all of you, or almost all of you, know that we live in that house which is called the bishop's house in such a manner as to imitate, as best we can, those saints of whom the Acts of the Apostles speaks: "No one called anything his own, but everything they had was in common" [Acts 4:32]. Since perhaps some of you are not such diligent observers of our life that you know it as well as I want you to, I will explain what I stated briefly.

I, whom in God's providence you recognize as your bishop, came to this city as a young man. Many of you know this. I was looking for a place to found a monastery and live with my brethren. I had given up all worldly hope, and did not wish to be what I could have been; but I did not seek to be what I am. "I chose to be the least in the house of my God rather than to dwell in the tent of sinners" [Ps 84:10]. I separated myself from those who love the world, but I did not place myself on a level with those who rule over peoples.

Nor did I choose a higher place at the banquet of my Lord, but a lower, unwanted one. And he chose to say to me, "Go higher" [Luke 14:10].

Until that time, I was so afraid of the office of bishop that I would not go to any place where I knew there was no bishop, because my reputation had begun to carry some weight among the servants of God. I was on my guard; and as much as I could I prayed in tears that I might find my salvation in a lowly station rather than be endangered in a high one. But, as I said, a servant should not contradict his lord. I came to this city to visit a friend, whom I though I could win for God and have live with us in our monastery. I felt safe, because there was a bishop here. I was seized; I was ordained a presbyter; and through this rank I came to the episcopate. I brought nothing. I came to this church with nothing but the clothes I was wearing at that moment.

And because I wanted to live in a monastery with my brethren, the elderly Valerius[28] of blessed memory, who understood my intention and my desire, gave me that garden where the monastery now stands. I began to gather brethren with the same good intention; poor, as I am; owning nothing, just as I owned nothing, and imitating me. Just as I sold my few possessions and gave the money to the poor, those who wanted to be with me were to do the same, so that we would live in common. God himself would be our great and precious common treasure.

I became a bishop. I realized that a bishop has to extend charity assiduously to whoever arrives or passes through; if a bishop did not do this, people would call him unkind. But it would have been improper to follow that practice in the monastery; and I wanted to have a monastery of clerics in the bishop's own house.

This is how we live. In our community no one may have anything of his own. Perhaps some do own something. But no one may. If any do own something, they are doing what is not allowed. But I have a good opinion of my brethren, and since I trust them I have avoided asking about this matter,

---

[28]Augustine's predecessor as bishop of Hippo Regius.

because even to ask would seem to me to be a kind of negative judgment. For I knew, and know, that all the men who live with me understand our way of life, and the law of our life.

3. The presbyter Januarius also came to us. What he appeared to own by right he gave away, and almost wholly disposed of, but not quite. He had some money left, that is, some silver, which he said belonged to his daughter. His daughter, by God's grace, is in the women's monastery and shows much promise. May the Lord guide her in fulfilling what we hope for her—in his mercy, not because of her merits. Because she was under the legal age and could not take charge of her own money—for although we admired her splendid dedication, we feared the fickleness of her young age—it was arranged that the silver itself would be kept for the girl, so that when she reached her majority she could act as a virgin dedicated to Christ should, at a time when she could do it best. Before she reached that age, he began to approach his death, and during that time made a will in his own name, not in his daughter's.

I repeat: this presbyter, our companion, who dwelt with us, was supported by the church, and professed common life, made a will. He made a will and appointed heirs. How painful to our company! This fruit was not borne by a tree which the Lord planted.

But—he named the church as his heir! I do not want those gifts. I do not like this bitter fruit. I sought him out for God. He joined our company. Let him keep to it, let him support it. He possessed nothing? He should not have made a will. He did own something? He should not have pretended to be our companion, like a man poor for God's sake.

Brethren, this is a great source of sorrow for me. I tell you, dear friends, on account of this sorrow I decided not to receive that legacy for the church. Let what he bequeathed pass to his children, let them do what they want with it. It seems to me that, if I accept it, I will be a participant in that act which displeases and pains me. I did not want to conceal this from you, my friends.

His daughter is in the women's monastery; his son is in the men's monastery. He disinherited both of them; in her case, with praise; in his case, with a clause of disinheritance, that is, censuring him. I recommended to the church that the children not receive those small inheritances, which disinherited children have a right to, until they reached their majority. The church keeps it for them.

Then a lawsuit arose between his children, and I am involved in it. His daughter says: "It is mine. You know that my father always said this." His son says: "My father should be trusted, because he could not have lied at the hour of death." What an evil dispute this is! And if the children themselves are dedicated to God, we can settle this strife between them quickly. I will hear them out like a father, and perhaps better than their own father. I will see what their disagreement is, and, as the Lord willed, I will hear the case between them along with some faithful and distinguished brethren from among your number, that is, from the people themselves, by God's grace, and as the Lord shall dispose, will put an end to it.

4. But I ask you for this: let no one reproach me because I do not want the church to receive this inheritance. First of all, I detest what Januarius did; and secondly, it is my own practice. Many praise what I am going to say, but some also find fault with it. It is very difficult to satisfy both parties. When the gospel was just being read, you heard the words: "We sang for you, and you did not dance; we lamented for you, and you did not grieve. John"—the Bapist—"came neither eating nor drinking, and they say, 'He has a demon'; the Son of Man came eating and drinking, and they say, 'Behold a glutton, a wine-drinker, the friend of tax collectors" [Matt 11:17-19]. What am I doing among those who are getting ready to pass judgment on me, and sink their teeth into me, if I receive the legacies of men who disinherit their own children in anger? Or what am I going to do for those for whom I sing, and they do not want to dance? Those who say: "See why no one gives anything to the church of Hippo; see why those who die do not make this church their heir—the bishop Augustine gives all of its property away, and accepts nothing." Their praise is biting; they flatter with their lips and sink in their teeth.

But I do accept things—I state publicly that I accept good

offerings, holy offerings. But in the case of someone who is angry with his son and disinherits him on his deathbed, would I not have calmed him down if he were alive? Ought I not to have reconciled his son to him? So how can I want him to be at peace with his son, if I am seeking his inheritance? It would be simple, if he did what I have often urged: that the man who has one child should consider Christ a second child; if he has two, let him consider Christ a third; if he has ten, let him make Christ the eleventh. Then I will accept the legacy. Because I did this in some cases, they now want to turn my generosity or the influence of my good name to another purpose, to blame me in another way because I am unwilling to accept the offerings of devout men. Let them think over how much I have accepted. What need is there to tally it up? I will mention just one: I accepted the legacy of Julianus's son. Why? Because he died without children.

   5. I did not want to accept the legacy of Bonifatius (or Fatius, as he was called)—not out of pity, but out of fear. I did not want Christ's church to be in the shipping business. There are many, of course, who make a fortune from shipping, too. But if there were one storm, if the ship sailed and were shipwrecked, would we have to hand men over to torture, so that an inquiry into the sinking could take place in the usual way? Those who were saved from the waves would be tortured by a judge. Would we hand them over? There is no way at all that the church ought to do this. Would the church therefore have to make restitution? How would it get the money? We may not hold capital in reserve. It is not right for the bishop to store up gold and push the beggar's hand away. So many ask, every day, so many weep, so many poor people beg, that we have to disappoint many of them because we do not have enough to give to all. And then we are supposed to keep a reserve in case of shipwreck? So I acted in this case by avoiding a gift, not by giving one. No one need praise this, but no one should censure it, either.

   It is clear that when I gave the son what his dying father, in his anger, had taken away from him, I did right. Those who wish to, may praise this act; I hope those, who do not wish to, will be forebearing. What more can I say, my brothers? If anyone wishes to gain an inheritance for the church at the expense of a disinherited son, let him find someone else to receive it; Augustine will not. By God's grace, I hope he would find no one. How praiseworthy was the act of the holy and venerable bishop Aurelius of Carthage! How he filled the mouths of all who knew him with the praises of God! A certain man had no children, and no hope of any. He gave all his possessions to the church, keeping only the income from the property for himself. He then had children; and the bishop returned his gift to the man, who hardly expected it. By right the bishop did not have to return the property—that is, under the law of the court, not the law of heaven.

6. Certainly, dear friends, you also know that I have said this to my brethren who dwell with me, that whoever possesses something should either sell it and give the proceeds away, or donate it, or make it common property; let the church, through which God cares for us, own it. And I allowed a delay, until Epiphany, for the sake of those who did not divide their property with their brethren and give it to them, or who had not yet done anything about their property because they were waiting for their legal age. Let them then do what they wish; but so long as they are poor with me, we shall look together for God's mercy.

But if they are unwilling, and perhaps some are unwilling—as you know, it is clearly I who had decided to ordain no cleric except one who wished to dwell with me— if someone should wish to free himself from this way of life, I would take his status as cleric away from him, because he was leaving the fellowship of our holy society which he had committed himself to and entered. Now behold: before God and before you, I change my decision: those who want to have their own property, for whom God and his Church are not enough, should remain where they want to, and where they can; I do not take their status as clerics away from them. I do not want hypocrites. This is bad; who doesn't know that? It is bad to lapse from a commitment; but it is worse to pretend to have one.

This is what I say: the man who deserts the fellowship of common life which he has once entered, and which the Acts of the Apostles praises, falls; he falls from his promise, he falls from his holy profession. Let him pay heed to a judge— but to God, not to me. I do not take away his status as a cleric. I have made clear to him how great the danger is; let him do what he wants. For I know that if I want to reduce in rank anyone who did this, he will not lack patrons, he will not lack partisans even among bishops. They would say, "What wrong has he done? He cannot bear that way of life in your company; he wants to live apart from the bishop, he wants to live on his own; should he lose the clerical rank for this reason?"

I know how bad it is to promise something holy and not fulfill it. "Make a vow," we read, "to the Lord your God and fulfill it" [Ps 76:11], and "It is better not to make a vow than to make one and not fulfill it" [Eccl 5:5]. Take, for example, a virgin: if she was never in a monastery, but is a consecrated virgin, she may not marry. She is not forced to live in a monastery. But if she enters a monastery, and then leaves, half of her intention is ruined, although she remains a virgin. In the same way, a cleric has promised two things: holiness, and the clerical state. Now God, through his people, imposes the clerical state on his shoulders; it is more of a burden than an honor (but "Who is the wise man who will understand this?" [Ps 107:43]). Therefore it is precisely holiness that he has promised. He promised to live in the fellowship of common life; he professed "how good it is and how blessed, for brothers to live as one" [Ps 133:1]. If he falls from this ideal, and living outside remains a cleric, half of him has fallen, What is this to me? I do not judge him. If he preserves his holiness outside, half of him has fallen. If he remains within hypocritically, he falls completely. I do not want him to have to be deceitful. I know how men love the clerical state; I take it away from no one unwilling to live with me in common. Whoever wishes to remain with me, possesses God. If he is ready to be supported by God through his Church, and not to own anything, but either to give what he owns to the poor or to share it in common, let him remain with me. Whoever does not want this may have his freedom; but let him see whether he can have an eternity of blessedness.

7. For the time being, let this suffice, dear friends. What I and my brethren will do—for I hope for good, I hope that all of them will freely obey me; I hope I will not find that some of them possess something, unless religion somehow demands it, not because greed occasions it—what I will do, I will announce to you, dear friends, after Epiphany; as God wills it. Nor will I conceal from you how I settle the case between the two siblings, the children of the presbyter Januarius. I have talked much. Please pardon my garrulous old age, and my fainthearted weakness. As you see, I have reached my old age. Because of my bodily weakness, I have now been an old man for a long time. But if what I have just said pleases God, he gives the strength; I do not desert you. Pray for me, that with whatever spirit there is in this body, and with whatever strength I have, I might serve you in God's word.

18. Siricius of Rome
Letter 1 (to Bishop Himerius)

Siricius was pope from 384 to 399. The letter translated here was written in 385 to Himerius, the bishop of Tarragona in Spain, and is interesting both for its content and its form. Himerius had addressed a series of questions to Pope Damasus, who however died (in 384) before he could answer them. The deacon Siricius was elected pope at the end of 384, and early in the following year answered Himerius's letter. Among other topics, Siricius promulgates regulations on clerical celibacy, on the advancement of clergy through the minor and major orders, and on the cooption of monks into the clergy. All show the growing tendency in the late fourth century to introduce detailed regulations for the clerical state and to add ascetical qualifications to it. The form of the letter is also important: it is the first extant papal letter in the style of a decretal, that is, a form taken over by the Roman curia from the imperial chancellery, originally used by the emperor to give authoritative and binding answers to questions posed by lower-ranking officials. For this reason, the letter is important in the history of the development of the papacy.

Siricius to Himerius, bishop of Tarragona.

1.[29] Because the Lord so willed it, your Fraternity's report, sent to our predecessor of holy memory, Damasus, reached me after I had already been elected to his see. When we read it through carefully at a meeting of the brethren, we found serious matters deserving of censure and correction, rather than the praiseworthy things we had hoped to learn. Since we had to succeed to Damasus's labors and concerns just as, by God's grace, we succeeded to his honor, after first appropriately informing you of my advancement, we do not deny you a suitable response to your inquiry, point by point, as the Lord deigns to favor us. Considering our office, we are not free to conceal anything or to keep anything secret, for a greater zeal for all the followers of the Christian religion is incumbent upon us. We bear the burdens of all who are weighed down—or rather, it is the blessed apostle Peter who bears them in our person, for we trust that he protects us in all the aspects of his ministry and watches over his heirs.

I.2. Therefore: at the very beginning of your letter you indicated that many persons who were baptized by the impious Arians are hurrying to the Catholic faith, and that some of our brethren wish to baptize them again. This is not permitted, for these reasons: the Apostle forbids this practice; the canons oppose it; and the general decrees sent to the provinces by my predecessor of venerable memory, Liberius, after the unsuccessful council of Rimini, prohibit it.[30]

---

[29]Text: PL 13.1132-1147.

[30]This council, in 359, was the emperor Constantius's last attempt to force Arianism on the West. Liberius's letter, written in 362, is not extant.

We receive these persons into the Catholic communion just as we do Novatianists and other heretics, as is decreed in the synod, only through the invocation of the sevenfold Spirit by the imposition of the bishop's hand. The whole East and West also retain this practice. Henceforth you should not deviate from this practice in any way, unless you wish to be cut off from communion with us by a synodal decision.

II.3. The next point is an objectionable confusion, and one which should be corrected, among candidates for baptism, when our fellow priests (and we are angry as we say this) dare to baptize at any time that pleases them, not based on any authority but only on indiscretion. Countless people, as you assert, receive the sacrament of baptism on Christmas Day, or on the Epiphany, or even on the feasts of apostles and martyrs with no discrimination or restriction, although this privilege belongs, both in Rome and in all the churches, particularly to Easter Sunday and to Pentecost, which accompanies it. It is only on these days of the year that the sacrament of baptism should be conferred collectively on those flocking to the faith—and then only on those candidates who have handed in their names forty days or more beforehand and who have completed the exorcisms, the daily prayers and the fasts, so that the apostolic precept might be obeyed, that once the old leaven has been purged, a new dough might begin to exist. On the one hand, therefore, we state that the holy reverence due to the pascal feast is not to be diminished in any way. On the other hand, we wish with all speed to help children who, because of their age, cannot yet speak, and those who need the water of holy baptism out of some necessity, lest it lead to the loss of our souls, if the saving waters are denied to those who want them and someone should depart from this world and lose both the Kingdom and life. Moreover, any who run the risk of shipwreck, an enemy's attack, the uncertainty of siege, or any incurable physical sickness, and who beg to be aided by this unique assistance of the faith, should receive the rewards of the new birth which they seek at the moment they ask for it. Let this suffice to correct the error in this matter; now let all the priests who do not wish to be sundered from the solidity of that apostolic rock upon which Christ built the universal Church keep the rule we have just stated.

III.4. The next point is that some Christian—it is terrible to say it—are going over to apostasy, and have been profaned by the worship of idols and the defilement of sacrifices. We order them to be cut off from the body and blood of Christ, which a short while ago had redeemed them and given them new birth. And if at some time they perhaps come to their senses and are converted to penitence, they are to do penance for their whole lives, and be given the grace of reconciliation at the very end of their lives because, as the Lord teaches, we do not want the death of the sinner, but only that he be converted and live.

IV.5. You also asked about conjugal veiling, whether a man can receive in matrimony a girl betrothed to another. We prevent this in every way from being done because the blessing, which the priest bestows on a woman who is going to marry, is considered by the faithful to be profaned if it is violated by any transgression.

V.6. Your Charity thought rightly that the apostolic see should be consulted concerning those who once performed penance and then, like dogs returning to their former vomit, and swine to their wallowing-places, have sought out the military belt, and the pleasures of the theater, and new marriages. They have entered forbidden unions, and their children, begotten after they received absolution, made public their manifest incontinence. Since these persons no longer have the choice of doing penance, we have decided to pronounce the following sentence: they should be united to the faithful within the church by prayer alone, and may be present at the sacred celebration of the mysteries, although they do not deserve this. But they must be separated from the fellowship of the Lord's table, so that they will be reproached at least by this penalty, and will both mend their own errors and provide others with an example to keep them back from filthy desires. But because they fell through the weakness of the flesh, we want them to be supported by the grace of communion, to serve as a viaticum, when they are about to go to the Lord. We judge that this same procedure should also be followed in regard to women who fell into such defilement after doing penance.

VI.7. Furthermore, you testify that some of the monks and nuns have rejected their commitment to holiness and have sunk into such licentiousness that they have lain together in illicit and sacrilegious intercourse, at first secretly, behind the walls of their monasteries; but then, led to the very brink of despair over their bad conscience, they freely begot children out of their forbidden embraces. Both public laws and ecclesiastical rules condemn this. We therefore order these shameless and detestible persons to be expelled from their monastic communities and from the assemblies of the churches, so that when they have been shut up in their workhouses and are bewailing their great sin in continuous laments, they might boil away in the purifying fire of repentance. At least at the moment of death, on grounds only of mercy, kindness may come to their aid by the grace of communion.

VII.8. Let us come now to the sacred orders of clerics. Your Charity states that we find that throughout your provinces they have been so scorned and disordered, to the harm of venerable religion, that we must speak in Jeremiah's own words: "Who will give water to my head, or a font of tears to my eyes? I will weep for this people day and night" [Jer 9:1]. If the blessed prophet says that his tears cannot suffice for weeping for the sins of the people, how much grief will dishearten us, when we are forced to weep for the crimes that exist in our own body—especially among those upon whom, according to the blessed Paul, daily intercession and concern for all the churches are an incessant obligation. "For who is sick, and I am not sick? Who is scandalized, and I do not burn?" [2 Cor 11:29]. For we have learned that very many priests of Christ, and deacons, after a long period of dedication, have begotten offspring, both from their own wives and also out of sinful unions, and defend their crime with this excuse, that in the Old Testament priests and ministers are given the right to procreate.

9. Now let that partisan of lust and teacher of vices, whoever he is, tell me this: if he judges that in the law of

Moses the reins of pleasure are indiscriminately relaxed by the sacred commandments of the Lord, why does he forewarn those to whom the Holy of Holies is entrusted, saying, "Be holy, because I the Lord your God am also holy"[Lev 20:7]? And why are the priests, in the year of their service, bidden to live in the temple, away from their homes? Obviously for this reason, that they could not have carnal intercourse even with their wives, and could therefore offer a gift acceptable to God, gleaming from the purity of their consciences. When they had finished the time of their service, the usual marriage customs were relaxed, but only for the sake of begetting offspring, because it was from no other tribe but the tribe of Levi that anyone was bidden to enter the service of God.

10. Whence the Lord Jesus, too, when he had enlightened us by his coming, declares in the Gospel that he came to fulfill the Law, not to abolish it. And so he desired the beauty of the Church, whose bridegroom he is, to be radiant with the brilliance of chastity, so that on the day of judgment, when he comes again, he can find her without spot or wrinkle, as he taught through his Apostle. All of us priests and deacons are bound by the indissoluble law of these decrees: from the day of our ordination we dedicate our hearts and bodies to temperance and chastity while in every way we please our God by these sacrifices which we offer daily. "Those who are in the flesh," says the Vessel of Election, "cannot please God. But now you are not in the flesh, but in the spirit, if the Spirit of God dwells in you" [Rom 8:8-9]. And where can God's Spirit dwell, as we read, except in holy bodies?

11. And since some of those we are speaking of, as your Holiness reports, lament the fact that they fell out of ignorance, we state that under the following condition they should not be denied mercy: so long as they live they should remain in the rank they held when they were found out, without any advancement in honor, but only if they commit themselves to remaining chaste thereafter. But those clerics who try to excuse their use of this forbidden privilege by claiming that it was granted to them by the Old Law should be informed that by the authority of the apostolic see they are stripped of every ecclesiastical honor, which they exercised unworthily; nor may they ever receive the venerable mysteries, which they have deprived themselves of by their lustful desires. And since these present cases forewarn us to be cautious in the future, let every bishop, presbyter and deacon know that, if he is subsequently discovered in this sin—which we hope will not happen—every path to forgiveness is closed to him from this moment on. Wounds must be cleansed with a knife when they do not respond to medicinal poultices.

VIII.12. We have also learned that men of unknown backgrounds, even those who have married several times, are boldly and openly aspiring to the aforementioned dignities, as it pleases each one. We bring this charge not so much against those who attain their offices through unbridled ambition, as particularly against metropolitan bishops who defy the commandments of our God, to the extent that they can, by closing their eyes to acts which are forbidden. To pass over in silence what we see as a higher ideal, where is that practice which our God established in the Law given through Moses when he said, "Let my priests marry once,"[31] and in another place, "Let a priest marry a virgin as his wife, not a widow or a rejected woman or a prostitute" [Lev 21:13-14]? The Apostle, the persecutor who became a teacher, followed it when he ordered that both the priest and the deacon ought to be "the husband of one wife" [1 Tim 3:2]. All of these precepts are so despised by the bishops of your districts that one would think that they commanded the opposite. And because we must not be negligent in treating transgressions of this sort, lest the righteous voice of an angry Lord reproach us with the words, "You saw a thief and you ran with him, and you threw in your lot with adulterers" [Ps 50:18], we decree by general proclamation what must in the future be followed by all the churches and what must be avoided.

IX.13. Whoever has dedicated himself to the service of the Church from his early childhood should be baptized before

---

[31]Not found in this form in the Old Testament.

the years of puberty and given the rank and ministry of lector. If he lives honorably from the beginning of adolescence until his thirtieth year, and is satisfied with only one wife—and if he married her when she was a virgin, and their marriage was blessed by a priest—he ought to be an acolyte, and a subdeacon. Afterwards, if he first shows that he is worthy by living continently, let him advance to the rank of diaconate. When he has served well as a deacon for more than five years, it is right for him to obtain the presbyterate. Thereupon, after a ten-year period, he can attain the episcopal chair, if the integrity of his life and faith is demonstrated throughout this time.

X.14. But a man who is already advanced in age and, summoned by a call to a better way of life, is eager to advance from the lay state to the sacred service, will not attain his goal and his wish in any other way except by numbering him immediately among the lectors and the exorcists at the time he is baptized, on the condition that, as an established fact, he had or has one wife, and that she was a virgin when he married her. After he has begun his service, two years should pass. For another five years let him be an acolyte and a subdeacon, and thus advance to the diaconate if, throughout this period, he is judged worthy. Then, having passed through these stages in good time, he will not be unworthy to attain the presbyterate or the episcopate, if the choice of the clergy and the people should fall upon him.

XI.15. Indeed, any cleric who marries either a widow or a second wife should immediately be stripped of every privilege of ecclesiastical dignity, and he may receive communion only in the rank of a layman. He may only keep this privilege if he does nothing thereafter for which he might lose it.

XII.16. We allow no other women to be in the houses of the clergy except those whom the Nicene synod allowed to dwell with them for reasons of necessity only.[32]

---

[32]Canon 3 of the Council of Nicaea (325) reads: "The great Synod stringently forbids any bishop, presbyter or deacon, or any one of the clergy, to have a woman dwelling with him, except a mother, or sister, or aunt, or such persons only as are beyond all suspicions."

XIII.17. We also desire and want monks to be added to the ranks of the clergy, if the dignity of their lives and their holy education in the faith recommend them. It should be done thus: monks who are less than thirty years old should be advanced in the minor orders, rank by rank, as the time passes, and thus they may attain the distinction of the diaconate and the presbyterate by the dedication of their mature years. They are not to ascend to the highest rank, the episcopate, in one step, but in their case also the same intervals which we have established above for each rank shall be observed.

XIV.18. It was also suitable for us to provide for this case: just as none of the clergy may perform public penance, so after penance and reconciliation no layman may every attain clerical rank; for, although they are cleansed from the contagion of their sins, they should not receive the instruments for celebrating the sacraments, since they had once been vessels of iniquity.

XV.19. Since only ignorance is offered as an excuse for all these faults which are censured, out of respect only for piety, we must sometimes mercifully pardon that ignorance. Any man who married a second time, or any who married a widow, and entered the sacred service unduly or improperly, should know that we grant him pardon under this condition, that he consider it a great benefit if, once all hope of advancement is taken from him, he may remain forever fixed at the rank at which he is found. The ranking bishops of all the provinces will know henceforth that, if they believe that any one of such men should be advanced to sacred orders, appropriate sentence will be passed by the apostolic see both against their own office and against the office of those whom they advanced in opposition to the canons and to our prohibition.

20. I believe, dearest Brother, that we have treated all the matters which were related in your complaint; and, as I see it, we have given adequate answers to the individual cases which you referred to the Roman church as to the head of your body through our son, the presbyter, Bassianus. Now we stir up your Fraternity's heart ever more faithfully to obey the canons and to keep the decretals we have laid down, so that you will bring the answers we have given to your inquiries to the attention of all our fellow bishops, and not only those who are by right in your diocese; and let these decisions which we have made through our good offices be sent, with a covering letter from you, also to all the bishops of the provinces of Carthaginensis, Baetica, Lusitania and Gallaecia,[33] and to those who border upon the nearby provinces to either side of you. And although no priest of the Lord is free to ignore the decisions of the apostolic see or the venerable canonical decrees, still it will be more practical, and a distinguished honor from your Charity in light of the long years of your priesthood, if the decisions sent to you by name but meant for all could be brought to the attention of all our brethren through your Unanimity's care. The salutary dispositions we have made, not unadvisedly but prudently, with great caution and extensive consultation, should remain unviolated, and the doorway to all future excuses, which can now be opened to no one among us, must remain blocked. Given on the third day before the Ides of February, in the consulship of Arcadius and Bauto.[34]

[33]With Tarraconensis, Himerius's province, the five Roman provinces which are now Spain and Portugal.

[34]That is, 11 February 385.

SUGGESTIONS FOR FURTHER READING

Audet, Jean-Paul. *Structures of Christian Priesthood.* New York, 1968.

Bastian, Ralph J. *Priesthood and Ministry.* Guide to the Fathers of the Church, 5. Glen Rock, 1969. (An anthology of short passages from the Fathers.)

Brown, Raymond E. *Priest and Bishop: Biblical Reflections.* New York, 1970.

Campenhausen, Hans von. *Ecclesiastical Authority and Spiritual Power in the Church of the First Three Centuries.* Tr. by J. A. Baker. Stanford, 1969.

Idem, "The Origins of the Idea of the Priesthood in the Early Church." In his *Tradition and Life in the Church,* pp. 217-230. Tr. by A. V. Littledale. Philadelphia, 1968.

Danielou, Jean. "The Priestly Ministry in the Greek Fathers." In *The Sacrament of Holy Orders,* pp. 116-126. London and Collegeville, 1962.

Davies, J. G. "Deacons, Deaconesses and the Minor Orders in the Patristic Period." *Journal of Ecclesiastical History* 14 (1963), 1-15.

Dix, Gregory. "The Ministry of the Early Church." In *The Apostolic Ministry*, pp. 183-303. Ed. by K. E. Kirk. 2nd ed.: London, 1957.

Eastwood, Cyril. *The Royal Priesthood of the Faithful: An Investigation of the Doctrine from Biblical Times to the Reformation.* Minneapolis, 1963.

Erhardt, Arnold. *The Apostolic Ministry.* Scottish Journal of Theology, Occasional Papers no. 7. Edinburgh, 1958.

Idem, *The Apostolic Succession in the First Two Centuries of the Church.* London, 1953.

Grant, Robert M. *The Apostolic Fathers: A New Translation and Commentary.* Vol. I: *An Introduction.* New York, 1964. (Ch. VI has an extended treatment of ministry.)

Greenslade, S. L. "Scripture and Other Doctrinal Norms in Early Theories of the Ministry." *Journal of Theological Studies* 44 (1943), 162-176.

Gy, P. M. "Notes on the Early Terminology of Christian Priesthood." In *The Sacrament of Holy Orders*, pp. 98-115. London and Collegeville, 1962.

Hertling, Ludwig. *Communio: Church and Papacy in Early Christianity.* Tr. by Jared Wicks. Chicago, 1972.

Iersel, Bas van, and Murphy, Roland, eds. *Office and Ministry in the Church.* Concilium, 80. New York, 1972.

Kilmartin, Edward J. *The Eucharist in the Primitive Church.* Englewood Cliffs, 1965.

Luttenberger, G. H. "The Decline of Presbyteral Collegiality and the Growth of Individualization of the Priesthood (4th-5th Centuries)." *Recherches de Théologie ancienne et médiévale* 48 (1981), 14-58.

Idem, "The Priest as a Member of a Ministerial College: The Development of the Church's Ministerial Structure from 96 to c. 300 A.D." *Recherches de Théologie ancienne et médiévale* 43 (1976), 5-63.

Meslin, Michel. "Ecclesiastical Institutions and Clericalization from 100 to 500 A.D." In *Sacralization and Secularization*, pp. 39-54. Ed. by Roger Aubert. Concilium, 47. New York, 1969.

Meyer, Charles R. "Ordained Women in the Early Church." *Chicago Studies* 4 (1965), 285-308.

Mohler, James A. *The Origin and Evolution of the Priesthood: A Return to the Sources.* Staten Island, 1970.

Ryan, Laurence. "Patristic Teaching on the Priesthood of the Faithful." *Irish Theological Quarterly* 29 (1962), 25-51.

Telfer, W. *The Office of a Bishop.* London, 1962.